The Table Rocks of Jackson County: Islands in the Sky

Compiled and edited
by
Chris Reyes

Last Minute Publications
Ashland

B+Noble   May 2004   Botany Club

To those who encourage the dreams of others.

Independent Printing Company, Ashland, Oregon.
Designed by DMI, Grants Pass, Oregon.

Library of Congress Catalog Card Number #93-91595
ISBN 0-9637486-0-2

ACKNOWLEDGEMENTS

This project would not have been possible without certain individuals giving of their time, expertise and perhaps more importantly, trust to a stranger of unknown character!

Darren Borgias, Southwest Oregon Stewardship Ecologist of The Nature Conservancy, supplied the initial encouragement, interviews, and available resource material.

Thanks to the Stewardship Committee for giving me an audience.

Thanks to Joan Seevers and Julia Duggan of the Bureau of Land Management.

Frank Lang, Stewart Janes, Gerry Capps, and Alan St. John were contacted "out of the blue" and gladly lent their help for this project. I felt both Professors treated me with as much respect as one of their Master degree students!

The nurturers' of this manuscript, Dorothy and Irvine Schueller, allowed me to take over their computer room for the three years it took to complete this! If having me underfoot was one thing, they also included me for dinner (was it coincidence that it was my best time to work?) and kept me well supplied with the "brain foods": cookies, ice cream and coffee!! They allowed me to deride their IBM in moments of frustration! They introduced me to their neighbor Frank Darnell, a professor and consultant, who would drop everything to come over and help me retrieve lost files from ASCII land! (Thank you to his wife Fran also!)

Thanks to my friends and co-workers who gave me constant encouragement and listened patiently as this project progressed! Those who provided help, contacts, or accompanied me on the hikes, besides those pictured inside, were: Esther (my initial proofreader) and Gerry Corcoran, Richard Swaney, Drs. Don Turcke and Phil Grimm, Este Criswell, Shauna Kerr, Jan Grace, and Mark Klemczak. Jan and Mark also loaned me photographic equipment. JeriAnn Bonnici King was the first stockholder of Last Minute Publications. Bob Corcoran took time out from building his home to fly this nervous photographer over the Rocks, humorously dodging the commercial airline traffic.

Ed and Roberta Reyes, my parents, provided monetary assistance at a critical point, proving they took me seriously! (Hi, Mom!)

Dr. John Hewitt and Alan St. John helped with book cover design possibilities. Thanks for your time!

Thanks to all the local authors who graciously shared their experience with publishing! Art Bernstein inspired the title, check *76 Day-Hikes*, page 92.

Total strangers stopped to lend advice, such as Joe Shelton. He identified plants for us, and taught me how to pronounce *lomatium* and *brodiaea*.

Thanks, Ingrid Mauer of DMI; you made the design phase fun and I appreciate your attention to detail! Camille Showalter of Verbatim helped clean up my grammar. Cheryl Perry of IPCO gave my small project large-account treatment!

Thank you, Lois Smith, the Real Table Rock Lady, for all your time and care for this area and its people, and for your material you trusted me with.

ODE TO TABLE ROCK

V.A. Davis

Proud monarch of the lovely plain!
I salute thee, with rev'rent mein.
As morning beams,
Thy summit gleams,
And shadows with their clutching fingers
Climb thy steeps, while twilight lingers,
Soft o'er thy top,
Bold, Table Rock.

In the dim and distant ages,
Ere were turned history's pages,
Thy form appeared
All bleak and seared
Above the ocean's broken floor,
Amid the crash and awful roar,
Of earthquake's shock,
Grim, Table Rock.

Like some ruin old and hoary,
Silent, though crowned with glory
Thy tongue could tell,
Of what befell
Since order first from chaos sprung
And around thee man's reign had begun
That ne'er shall stop,
Rare, Table Rock.

From thy summit in days gone by
The savage viewed, with bodeful eye
His setting sun
Thy course shall run
Embalmed in story, old and stable,
Historic page, Indian fable,
And battle shock
Stern, Table Rock

When spring's green witchery like a loom,
Weaves the valley, in bud and bloom,
And birds and bees
Sweet harmonies
Charm the scene and entrance the skies,
Visions open of paradise,
Around thy top,
Grand, Table Rock!

The swallows come and swallows go,
Ever the river's crystal flow
Still seaward sweeps
Thy reign yet keeps
Unchanged amid our turbid life,
The ebbs and flows of human strife,
Concern thee not
Strong, Table Rock.

Noble mountain, so should we,
Adrift on life's unresting sea,
    With love ignored,
    Ambition lowered,
Take heart and brave the battling fates,
Grip hands with Hope, until the gates
    Of life unlock
    O, Table Rock.

"Professor" V.A. Davis taught at the Table Rock School 1905-06, 1910-1912, and 1930-31. Poem included in *An Early History of Table Rock,* by Katherine Nealon Huntress Leavitt, 1968. Reprinted with permission from the Southern Oregon Historical Society.

Table Rock School, Class of 1912. *Back Row:* Floyd Morgan, Clark Collins, Byron DeFord, Fay DeFord, Clara Collins, Dovie Patch, Lillian Canfield, Helen Lydiard, V.A. Davis, Maude Corlies. *Front Row:* Joe Collins, Katherine Nealon, Lydia DeFord, Pansy Conley, Juanita Hall, Rachel Wager, Bell Morgan, Mary Collins, Jennie Morgan, Ben DeFord, Cuma DeFord, Eva Nealon, Nellie Eldredge, Clarence Eldredge, Myrtle Byrum, Clifford Collins.

TABLE OF CONTENTS

LIST OF PHOTOGRAPHS AND ILLUSTRATIONS

Photographs

Photographs by Chris Reyes, except where indicated.

Color Plates

Illustrations

Maps

Maps by Chris Reyes, except where indicated.

Newspaper Articles

FOREWORD

The Rogue Valley is a geologic wonderland, with volcanic displays in nearly every direction one looks. Its diversity is startling, from pointy, conical peaks to old, rounded ranges. A huge, bare lava plug catches the eye at the south end of the valley, and twin mesas, seemingly out of Arizona, dominate the view at the north end.

These plateaus, the Table Rocks, have an intriguing presence that has drawn people since prehistoric times. Their cliffs are natural fortresses. One can imagine being upon an island, isolated, yet not too far from the sea of everyday life. Viewing the little details below is like looking into a tide pool: the Matchbox cars and trucks, the patchwork fields, the ribbon of the river.

Accessibility is a big part of The Rocks' appeal. They are right at our doorsteps. They both have quick, well-planned trails. There are signs directing the way. One does not need special clothes or equipment to climb there. They provide an equal-opportunity adventure, available to the young and old, the poor and rich, the unimpaired and the handicapped.

They are also islands of plant and animal communities (some of them rare or unusual) set in the midst of a desert, in the midst of civilization even. For this reason The Rocks have come to the attention of those with the means to preserve them. It is easy to take The Rocks for granted, as if they had always belonged to the public, which is not true even today.

The purpose of this handbook is to help interpret the sights and sounds of the Table Rocks, to tell some of the history that these two landmarks have witnessed around their skirts, to show how humans have affected this habitat, and to bring to light some of the preservation activities and to help identify who is involved. (Apologies to those who may have been left out, and thank you.)

This is the time to recall that The Rocks are fragile and can easily be abused. Due to caring preserve managers, conscientious hikers, and volunteer work days, there is little trash and vandalism seen. A lot of the abuse has not been made public. Increased interest means both increased use and increased threat. One cannot promote The Rocks without mixed emotion. I hope that awareness will bring greater responsibility and more conservation efforts.

Feel free to submit comments or information about the Table Rocks to Last Minute Publications.

Editor
P.O. Box 3332
Ashland, OR 97520

Children easily climb The Rocks. *From left:* Tammy Pecis, Melissa Reyes, Cheril Reyes.

"In early days the young people got their thrills from venturing over the cliffs of Table Rock." —Katherine Nealon Huntress Leavitt

Pioneer's playground. *Shown are:* Effie and Ellie Sage, John, Emmett and Mary Nealon, Blanche Collins and Eva Hall of the Table Rock community. Carl Beebe, Lorne Gregory and Tom Perdue of the Agate community. Alberta and Flora Stacy from the Antioch community. Cleve and John Wilson of Sams Valley. Lester Wertz from Eagle Point.

INTRODUCTION

In the early days, The Rocks were the locals' "playground." (Smith, L. 1992) Homes and driveways were far apart, and it was okay to cut across the neighbor's property to climb them. As population density increased, strained relations began between the hikers, clogging narrow roads with their cars, and the local landowners, who might have felt the territorial tug to protect their property. One access route required asking the family at the end of the road for permission! (Leavitt 1968) How many would gladly open their doors to strangers these days?

Landowners wanted to improve their property on the flanks of The Rocks by building roads and fences, clearing tangled chaparral areas, bringing in new plants and animals. At least a couple of landowners tried to make the mesa pay off by farming, mining, or building subdivisions upon it.

Today there is a careful balance between the government and private groups, landowners, and the public. There are lots of interests represented: scientific, educational, environmental, historical, and industrial, among others. Yet, it is still the hard work of relatively few that keep it this way!

Human Aspects of the Natural Area

The Rocks are cooperatively managed by The Nature Conservancy and the Medford District of the Bureau of Land Management. In the private sector, the Rogue River Ranch owns major portions of both Table Rocks and has grazing permits for Upper Table Rock.

The Nature Conservancy is a private, non-profit, international conservation organization. It was incorporated in 1951. Its mission is to protect biologic diversity by attempting to preserve "intact" natural habitats. It seeks out significant natural areas and gives them priority based on rare attributes (plants and animals) and threat of development. These properties are secured through gifts, lease or purchase, and then the Conservancy helps plan the stewardship of the area, involving government agencies and the public. Frequently, there are co-op projects where the Conservancy is able to buy an important land parcel and then hold it until the government agency can buy it or a land trade can be worked out. With creative, flexible, and intelligent strategy, the Conservancy attempts to save "the last great places." It has set aside approximately 15 million acres throughout the United States, Canada, and Latin America!

One of 51 natural area preserves in Oregon, totalling 212,831 acres, the Lower Table Rock Preserve has 1,871 acres. A Nature Conservancy ecologist is close by to provide biologic monitoring, research, and public education for all the preserves in his territory. Many preserves also have a Stewardship Committee to help make decisions for it.

Large portions of the summit of Upper and Lower Table Rock are owned by The Bureau of Land Management. The BLM is a federal land management agency, a branch of the Department of Interior. It oversees 300 million acres of public land and strives for multiple uses of them. This allows for timber sales, mining for minerals, leasing of range land, hunting and fishing areas, preservation of watersheds and, of course, recreation! It also recognizes areas of important natural and cultural resources and designates them Areas of Critical Environmental Concern (ACEC). Such areas are then specially managed to preserve the features for which they were nominated. Some 1,240 acres of Upper and Lower Table Rock are designated ACEC.

The Rogue River Ranch was established in 1982 by the Jake Wood family and produces Registered Polled Herefords, purebred breeding cattle. "The ranch supports use of the Table Rocks by graciously allowing the public on their land and by providing access for organized disabled drive-up tours on Upper Table Rock." (Borgias 1992) Ranch holdings are easily identified by the red roofs on its structures.

Other Notable Aspects

Two other areas surrounding The Rocks merit attention because of their relationship to them, the river, and for uniqueness of their own. They are Kelly Slough and the Agate Desert.

Kelly Slough is the backwater formed by Gold Ray Dam on the Rogue River, and is visible from the top of Lower Table Rock. It supports the largest stand of riparian (streamside) vegetation in southern Oregon, with its cottonwood forest harboring a large great blue heron rookery. This area was also included in the big preservation push for Lower Table Rock. About 477 acres are now public lands, 300 acres belonging to Jackson County (as part of the Bear Creek Greenway) and the rest to the Oregon Department of Fish and Wildlife. It is easy to forget this area is manmade,

Family Fairytale: Candie and John Steely told their children, Ashleigh *(right)* and Garrett *(left)* that giants sit down for dinner at the Table Rocks.

by construction of the dam around 1903. If the dam were removed, this stable environment would be destroyed. (Smith, K. 1993) Future plans for the area include an interpretive canoe trail.

Former river beds and gravel bars form the Agate Desert, named because rock hounds find petrified wood and other agatized material here. (Swisher, *Siskiyou Naturalist*) The desert has a surface that resembles the tops of the Table Rocks, with "patterned ground" and seasonal pools forming over the impermeable hardpan layer three feet below the surface. (Jackman and Bernstein 1989) The Nature Conservancy has a 49-acre preserve in the area. Several tracts of the desert comprise the Ken Denman State Game Management Area, which the Oregon Department of Fish and Wildlife oversees. There is also the Denman Interpretive Trail at TouVelle State Park.

"View from Table Rock" original caption, date unrecorded.

HOW, WHERE, WHEN AND WHAT:
Answers to Common Questions

How do we get to them?

It may seem obvious just to get on Table Rock Road and head toward The Rocks. There is a trick to it, but there are signs to point the way!

To find Table Rock Road:
Those driving on Interstate 5 can take either Medford Exit #30 (if heading north) or Central Point Exit #32 (north or south):

From Exit #30, turn left onto Biddle Road and drive for about two miles to the intersection with Table Rock Road. Turn right at the signal there.

From exit #32 at Central Point, turn left (if coming from the north) or east and head down the highway for about a mile to the intersection with Table Rock Road. Turn left.

From central Medford, Table Rock Road branches to the right off of North Pacific Highway, also known as Highway 99 North, at an intersection called the Big Y, at the northwest corner of the Rogue Valley Mall.

For Upper Table Rock: Drive 4.3 miles from the intersection of Biddle and Table Rock Roads to reach the green Bybee bridge (#164) crossing the Rogue River at TouVelle State Park. Approximately one mile past the Bybee Bridge, turn right onto Modoc Road. (It's near a sharp curve, and the green Table Rock Trail sign is visible.) Go about 1.5 miles and look for a small power substation on the right. The trailhead parking lot is on the left side of Modoc Road, across from it.

For Lower Table Rock: Proceed on Table Rock Road to the 10-mile marker. There is a green Table Rock Trail sign indicating a left turn onto Wheeler Road. Continue on Wheeler Road for a half-mile and the trailhead parking lot will be visible on the left.

Is one plateau higher than the other?

Although Upper Table Rock is slightly higher on one end, The Rocks were named for their relationship to the Rogue River. Hence, Upper Table Rock is "upstream" from Lower Table Rock. Both Rocks are roughly 800 feet high. The highest point on Upper Rock is 2,091 feet and the highest point on Lower is 2,049 feet.

How long are the trails and where do they go?

Upper Table Rock: This trail is approximately one mile long. I tend to recommend Upper Table Rock climb for first timers!

Upper's trail begins 150 feet higher up the skirt than Lower's trail, and it is approximately a half-mile shorter. Also, it is not so far across Upper's plateau, making it is quicker to reach the rim than on Lower Rock.

Upper Table Rock's trail is easy to follow, and it has a couple of turnouts that bring hikers back to the main trail. Do not step over obviously blocked paths and do not follow the almost healed-over jeep road.

Climbers come out on the edge of the Upper Rock's eastern arm. There are obvious trails across its top, one that leading over to the edge

1

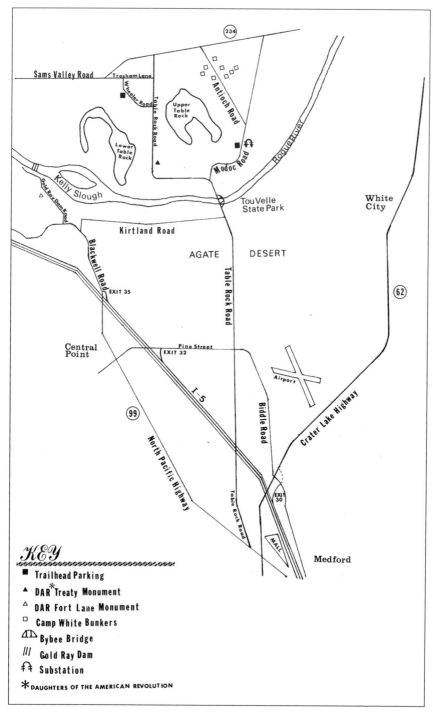

Finding the Trailheads.

looking across its "bowl" to the other arm, and another leading to the cliff that overlooks Modoc Road and the valley. There is also a faint jeep road that leads to the VOR aviation tower. The building is about a mile and a half away; it is farther than it looks!

Lower Table Rock: Lower Table Rock's trail is approximately one and a half miles long. There is a fork at the half-mile mark with a sign for the right fork (if vandals have not removed it) that reads "Bench Trail." The fork to the left is the main route, and it leads to the north end of the Lower Rock's eastward arm. It is approximately another mile to the south end to look over the valley. The remains of the former landing strip will be underfoot.

Those feeling adventurous should try the right fork, which is a longer and *slightly* more rigorous route. True to the sign, there are three benches to rest on along the way! This route goes over the shoulder of The Rock about 100 feet from

Irvine Schueller contemplates the view from a bench along Upper Table Rock's trail.

the top (another kind of "bench"), and descends to a dirt road. Reclimb to the top following this jeep road (which is briefly on private property). I had to bushwhack some of the way due to overgrown vegetation. Even though this alternate route gave me some new scenery, I felt lost.

How long should this take us?

I would plan for *at least* three to four hours for either hike.

When should we go?

Everyone knows the answer to this: Springtime, of course! March through June has the best show of wildflowers, with April being the peak of the season.

It is estimated that 7,000 to 10,000 people visit the Table Rocks annually. I hope, though, that we do not all go on the same day!

Spring The flowers wake up in ever increasing waves. The kinds of flowers seem to change weekly. It reaches a peak and then the flowers retreat as the water becomes less available. Around the drying vernal pools are rings of small blue flowers, downingia. Everything fades to a golden brown.

The effect is underwhelming to some, though...A coworker, who anticipated his first climb for weeks, exclaimed that the flowers were SO SMALL!

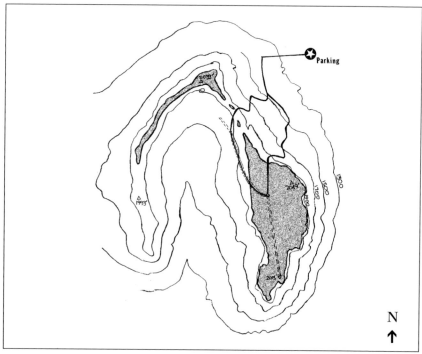

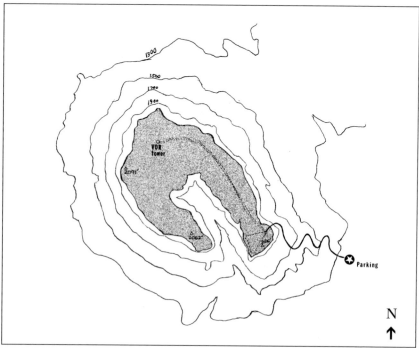

Lower and Upper Table Rock Trails.   *(Not to scale.)*

Summer and Fall I had heard that there is always something blooming on The Rocks all year, but one must look very hard late in the summer.
The Rocks also have a reputation for being rattlesnake-ridden at that time,
and while it is true those guys love it up there, it is very difficult to run
across one. Poison oak and ticks are the main enemy, says John Ifft, formerly of the BLM, who did not see a rattler the whole time he was helping
to build Lower's trail.

My experience hiking Upper Table Rock in late August was not
unpleasant, but one must be prepared for scruffiness. The grasses were
very dry, and the woodland community gave me literally a "red carpet"
reception: the madrones were shedding their bark like old sunburns and it
mixed on the ground with scraps of other red leaves, no doubt poison oak!
I was tense the whole way up, expecting a rattler to be lying along the
path. It was so quiet that I could hear the tiniest insects creeping. The top
of The Rock appeared to me, with an untrained eye, to be mostly star thistle and dry grasses, yet I did find purple vinegar weed and yellow spike-
weed. Yellow-flowered rabbitbrush grew in interesting dusty blue-green
tufts at the cliff edges.

I got an adrenaline rush after I had relaxed my guard and almost
stepped on a squirrel who was hiding in a depression beside the trail. At
the same moment as he bolted and barked expletives, a hawk startled off a
branch overhead. It was a moment later that I realized that I had stumbled
into a life-and-death moment of the food chain, and I did not know for
which one to feel the most sorry!

Winter Wintertime brings foggy vistas, slick trails, and the vernal
pools. Art Bernstein mentioned in *76 Day-Hikes* of seeing flocks of ducks
at the pools. The mosses and
selaginella (a moss-like plant) are
actually green, and there are tiny
mushrooms about.

Just for the sake of seeing The
Rocks in all their seasons, I recently
climbed Upper after a snowfall. On
sections of the trail covered with
snow, the tracks of the only other visitors could be seen: deer, and what I
hoped was a local dog's. On the
summit, all the rocky rubble had caps
of snow, even in the vernal pools.
On the cliffs, the trickle of thousands
of tiny waterfalls could be heard as
the snow melted. There were spec-
tacular clouds overhead, and I could
see the reflection of hundreds of little
ponds all over the valley floor. I did
not do the trail any favors, though.
On the walk back down, I slipped
and slid and left large clods of mud
everywhere.

Chris Reyes becomes fogbound on
Upper Table Rock in January.

What should we bring?

This is my personal list, and I am one of those overly careful persons that Thoreau said would bring a medicine chest huckleberrying! You can zoom up and down The Rocks without bringing anything. I have met two men who walk them at least twice a week for exercise, and they travel light!

- ❏ comfortable shoes or boots
- ❏ water (there is none available)
- ❏ toilet paper (Pack it out! See page 119)
- ❏ camera & tripod
- ❏ binoculars
- ❏ fanny pack
- ❏ lunch (my favorite!)
- ❏ walking stick
- ❏ hat
- ❏ bug repellent (ticks, hungry mosquitoes during a wet spring)
- ❏ first-aid kit (a few band-aids in a ziploc bag will do, you may want to include some "Wet-wipes" to clean off poison oak mishaps)
- ❏ layered clothing (it's nice and warm climbing the trails, then it can be chilly from the wind on the summit)

What else should we know?

These are guidelines set up by the Table Rock Stewardship Committee to prevent damage to the Preserve. By honoring these, we can all be considered stewards:

•Beware of the dangers: high cliffs, poison oak, ticks, rattlesnakes, primitive trails, and no water.

•Stay on the trails to avoid excess erosion and disturbing vegetation. Certain sections are closed for restoration.

•The interior valleys, or "bowls," are not open to public use.

•Do not pick the flowers! A picked flower cannot reproduce future generations.

•Avoid walking on the soft ground near vernal pools. The soil here is especially sensitive to disturbance.

•Do not disturb vegetation, wildlife, or scientific study plot markers.

•Dogs are not allowed in order to prevent disturbing ground nesting birds and other animals.

•Horses are not allowed in order to reduce erosion of the trail, reduce the spread of non-native plants, and prevent unsafe interactions with pedestrians.

•Bikes and other vehicles are not allowed.

•No hunting or firearms allowed.

•No camping and no fires.

•Please pick up trash and remove it from the area. (From *Table Rock Interpretive Guide*—Borgias 1992)

Talent man falls to death while seeking firewood on Table Rock

A Talent man died late Saturday in a fall while searching for firewood on Upper Table Rock, Jackson County sheriff's deputies said.

Gary Carl Corbin, 33, of 1962 Pioneer Road, was pronounced dead at 11 p.m. when he was found by searchers called by Corbin's companions.

The four companions told deputies Corbin had gone to gather wood for a bonfire at 6 p.m., shortly after sunset. His friends did not see him fall, but heard a loud noise of broken tree limbs and falling rocks.

When they realized Corbin was missing, and could not see him from a viewpoint, they hiked down the mountain and went to the TouVelle Food and Brew to call for help. Dispatchers received the call at 8:10 p.m., sheriff's Lt. Ed Mayer said. Jackson County,

Central Rogue and Western Rogue Search and Rescue organizations responded with 11 volunteers and equipment.

The teams began searching for Corbin on the southwest slope of the mesa at 10 p.m, and found him at 11 p.m. He had fallen about 60 feet down a steep slope, rolled off a slight ledge and fallen another 35 feet onto a tree limb, Mayer said.

How is the weather?

The Rogue Valley climate is classified as Mediterranean: mild year-round, with a rainy season and a period of drought. Because the Klamath Mountains form a barrier to wet coastal clouds, the valley floor only receives around 18 inches of rain per year. The temperature range is usually between 32-100 degrees F, with rare drops below 0 degrees. The valley floor occasionally receives some snow, but it rarely lasts for more than a day. Residents know the valley can cook above 100 degrees for a week at a time during the late summer. The hot days have very low relative humidity. Watch for thunderstorms during the summer. Winds are usually light, averaging less than 6 miles an hour 80 percent of the days. They usually prevail from the south and southwest during the winter and from the northwest during the summer. Low wind speed is part of the famous Rogue Valley air inversion problem, with the valley being socked in fog and air pollution during the winter. There is often a "false spring" in February, with beautiful sunny days to tempt one out of the house.

How did they get the name—Table Rocks?

Who first used "Table Rock" is still a mystery. It did not seem to be the first white man to traipse around the valley, Peter Skene Ogden of Hudson's Bay Company fame. In his journals from this 1827 trek, he never once mentioned these two landmarks! (LaLande 1987) Table Rock is such a common name for this type of formation! There is a Table Rock in the Salem area. When posed this question, Jeff LaLande, local archeologist, historian, and author, thought that it may have been either the French Hudson Bay Company trappers who named them (they named the Rogue River) or the first American settlers. Early maps did not include such small details. A detachment of the U.S. Exploring Expedition came through in 1841, but the Wilkes journal did not mention them either. The party was weakened by illness and feared an Indian attack, and the valley was filled with smoke at the time.

In 1845, a party of emigrants passed through the Rogue Valley, and mountain man James Clyman made mention of the Table Rocks. (Beckham 1971)

The local Indians, the Takelma, had a large winter encampment near Lower Table Rock. (See *The First Ones*) Their name for the area was Titanakh, meaning little Indian plums. (Gray 1987) Table Rock proper may have been Di'tani, meaning "rock above." (Card 1967) I have to wonder if the Takelma used tables or even had a word for them! Indian lands were reduced to the Table Rock Reservation, which was in place for three years beginning in 1853.

Jacksonville was first named Table Rock City in the early 1850's. Southern Oregon's first newspaper, published in Jacksonville by William G. T'Vault, was named the *Table Rock Sentinel*. (*Table Rock Sentinel* is now the name for the bimonthly publication of the Southern Oregon Historical Society.)

What landmarks are seen from the summits?

Mt. McLoughlin—9,495 ft. The conical volcano seen looking east. Named in honor of Dr. John McLoughlin, chief factor of the Hudson's Bay Company, officially in 1905. First called McLoughlin on a map of 1838, but later called Mt. Pitt. (Popularized in 1864—For the Pitt River and the Indian-dug game traps.) (Mc Arthur 1992) Other names have been Snowy Butte or Pitt's Peak.

Wagner Butte—7,265 ft. Named for the Jacob Wagner family, early pioneers. Looking south, it blocks the view of Mt. Ashland.

Pilot Rock—5,914 ft. The remains of an old volcano, called a volcanic neck or lava plug. Seen looking south from Upper Table Rock. Made a natural marker for the way over the Rogue/Klamath divide (Siskiyou Summit) since prehistoric times. Briefly named Emmons Peak, for Lt. George Emmons of the U.S. South Seas Surveying and Exploring Expedition of 1841. Takelmas called it "Tan-ts'at-seniphtha" or "Stone stand up." (Mc Arthur 1992)

Roxy Ann Peak—3,571 ft. Large rounded knoll east of middle of valley (looking south from The Rocks). Named in honor of Roxy Ann Bowen, who with husband John were settlers in the area around 1850. (Mc Arthur 1992)

The Rogue River—Named "La Riviere Aux Coquins" by the French trappers describing the local Indians. "Les Coquins" means "The Rogues"! In an 1833 Journal of the Hudson Bay Company, John Work called it River Coquin. In old Donation Land Claims, it's called Gold River. The territorial legislature officially named it Gold River in January 12, 1854. Changed back permanently to Rogue River in 1855. Takelmas called it Trashit. (Mc Arthur 1992)

What is the name of that rare flower up there?

It is the dwarf wooly meadowfoam, or *Limnanthes floccosa ssp. pumila* (See page 102). It is found only on the tops of the two Table Rocks, in the vernal pool areas, and nowhere else in the world. Its blooming period is for just about 10 days in April, so it is easy to miss.

In 1962, NASA sent Howard Gentry from the Department of Agriculture here to check out this little plant's seeds. It seems that the oil from the seeds is highly resistant to heat, a quality necessary for lubricating space vehicles. The fact that it is also self-pollinating means that the seed crop does not have to depend on bees. (Latimer 1990)

Researchers at Oregon State University are working with another meadowfoam, one found in the Agate Desert. This particular one, the *ssp. grandiflora*, could be a potential replacement for the sperm whale oil used in sensitive machinery. (Kranz and Richter 1980) Researchers are working to develop hybrids.

Because of the meadowfoam's unique gene pool, it is a federally recognized threatened species.

Which rock has the airstrip?

Lower Table Rock used to have an airstrip, with a windsock even! It was built by John Day, but was until recently maintained and used by the Experimental Aircraft Association. The EAA is a worldwide organization for owners of homebuilt aircraft or of single engine planes who are interested in sport or recreational flying.

The airstrip made a convenient path to walk on, yet it was easy to forget that planes had the right-of-way to land there.

The lease was not renewed with the BLM in 1990 because of liability insurance concerns. The Nature Conservancy is investigating ways to help return the landing strip area to its natural state.

So what is that building on top of Upper Rock?

It is the Federal Aviation Administration VOR Building. VOR stands for Very High Frequency Omni-Directional Range. (Bork 1978) It is basically a radio compass. The FAA maintains the building year-round and has a private gravel road that goes up the west side. It is not open to the public.

VOR Building on top of Upper Table Rock.

What is that monument beside Table Rock Road?

This is a historical marker placed by the Daughters of the American Revolution (DAR) in 1928. It commemorates the signing of the Treaty With the Rogue River, 1853 (See *Appendixes B* and *D*). The monument is located between the 9- and 10-mile markers, just after the sharp L curve, on the Upper Table Rock side of the road.

Another historical marker associated with the Table Rocks is on the site of Fort Lane. This monument was also erected by the DAR. Stones for the marker were gathered from the area of the fort. It is located on Gold Ray Dam Road, across the river from Lower Table Rock. Watch for a huge snag full of woodpecker holes, at approximately seven-tenths of a mile on the left. (See Map, page 2.)

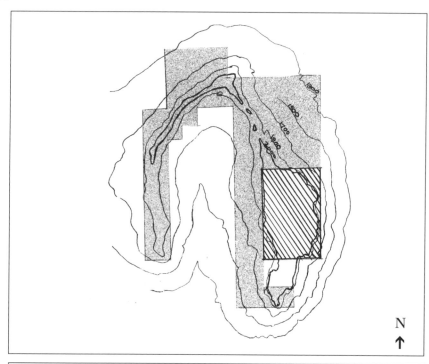

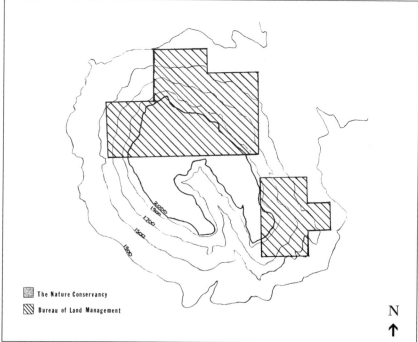

Lower Table Rock Preserve and Area of Critical Environmental Concern. *(Not to scale.)*

How big is the preserve?

Lower Table Rock is considered the Preserve (See *Introduction*), but the managed natural area of both Rocks is 3,300 acres. (Seevers and Borgias 1993)

Did the Indians jump off the cliffs?

The only tale I found regarding this comes from John Beeson's *A Plea For The Indians*, written in 1857:

"Two women and a man who had taken refuge upon Table Rock, which is high and very precipitous were pursued; and it was reported that they had killed themselves by jumping down its steep and craggy sides. But Dr. Ambrose, who lived in the vicinity, informed me that they fell because they were shot, and could not avoid it."

He goes on to describe that they were still alive at the base of The Rock. Reportedly, several prominent citizens, having witnessed this, wrote to Governor Curry to protest such outrages against peaceable Indians.

Table Rock Treaty Monument.

"...her dress was a mantle of antelope or deer skin, and cup shaped cap, made of rushes. She had a large funnel shaped basket which they all carry to collect roots and seeds in." —Titian Ramsay Peale, artist-naturalist with the U.S. Exploring Expedition of 1841, describing an Indian seen near present-day Ashland.

Indian woman with burden baskets.

THE FIRST ONES—A Cultural History

Up until the late 1850's a unique, stone-age people climbed these bluffs and lived in their shadows below. They were relatively unaware of the world outside their rugged valleys, trading with just their closest neighbors, and sometimes fighting with those same neighbors. Time's only significance for them was the cycle of food gathering for the winters. That is, until the white men began filtering through the valley. Then the race for survival became acute, as things changed daily for the native people. Their story is as interesting and tragic as any of the famous Midwest Indian tribes.

They were the Takelma, or Da-Gel-Ma, translated "those living alongside the river." (The name seems to be spelled Takilma in Josephine County) There were two main groups: the Upland or Lat-ga-wa Takelma, and the Lowland Takelma. The Takelma language is classed with the Penutian peoples, but has no close relatives. (Sapir said, "Takelma stands entirely isolated amongst its neighbors." Quoted from *Valley of the Rogues*) Penutian speakers were found in central California and Alaska, and it is thought that the language may have spread from Oregon. (*The First Oregonians* 1991) The Penutian migration brought the Takelma ancestors into the Rogue Valley approximately 5,000 years ago, although the oldest artifacts found date from 500 to 1,500 A.D. (Aikens, *Living with the Land*, 1990 and Bondinell 1979)

The Uplanders lived in the main Bear Creek drainage area: from the Ashland area to the Rogue River. They were considered the rougher people, poorer, cruder and more warlike, by their Lowland kin.

The Lowlanders lived along the northern bank of the Rogue River from Gold Hill up to Grants Pass. They also lived along the Illinois River and Galice Creek.

For a third division, a northern group with a slightly different dialect of Takelma lived along the Upper Rogue, in the Trail and Elk Creek area. These were referred to as the Ha-ne-sakh's or "rotten log people." (Gray 1987)

Living around and amongst the Takelmas were the Da-ku-be-te-de or Applegate Band , and the Tal-tuc-tun-te-de or Galice Creek Band. These tribes were of the Athapascan people, which is a huge linguistic family found from Alaska to Arizona.

Other neighbors, to the east and south, were the Shastas, of yet another linguistic stock, the Hokan-Sioun. There is evidence the Shastas lived in the Ashland area.

These "tribes"* were sometimes all lumped together as the Rogue River Indians. In this text, especially in describing the Indian Wars, the Rogue name will be interchanged with the Takelma.

Physical Features

The men were described as sturdy, averaging 5'8" tall and having great athletic endurance. They had large, oval faces with the classic prominent cheekbones, and "keen, bright eyes." (Heckert 1977) Women were shorter, with smaller features and lighter skin tone. One of the first visitors to the

---

*Tribe is not quite an accurate description since each village was an individual entity and were not united as a "nation."

13

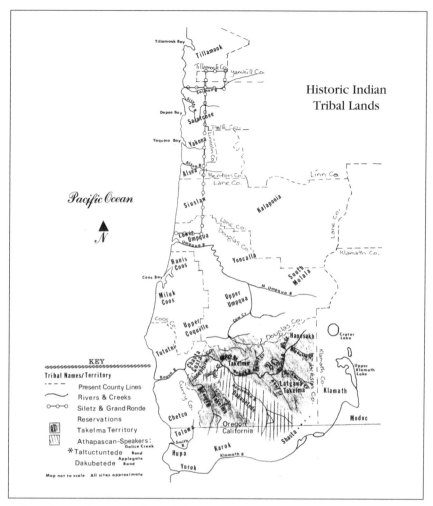

valley, Peter Skene Ogden of the Hudson's Bay Company, described the people as "wild and shy." (Heckert 1977)

Both genders had pierced noses and ears, in which they wore shells, bones or buckskin thongs. Women may have had chin tattoos: three vertical lines from lower lip to chin, made by scratching in charcoal and plant juices. Men were tattooed also, but only on their arms and hands, to measure strings of money shells (dentalia). Body paint was sometimes used. Red, black, and white were the only colors, however, white was only used for war paint. The Takelma tended to put vertical stripes on their chins and horizontal bars on their cheeks. Painting the forehead white was symbolic of the grizzly bear, which has a blaze of white above the eyebrows. This was done to receive the help and strength of the grizzly spirit. (Bondinell 1979)

Women wore straight bangs, and tended to part their hair down the back and wrap the sections at the side with strips of skins, sometimes decorated with dentalia. They did not braid their hair. Men wore their hair like the women, but twisted it up in a knot during battles. They also wore headbands. Special headbands were made with red woodpecker feathers.

The men wore a deerskin apron and one-piece moccasins during the warm months. Women wore knee length skirts made of deerskin or shredded bark fabric and covered their upper bodies with hide capes. They favored the round basket hat which was imported from the Shastas or Karoks.

Men owned a type of armor made of thick, woven sticks or stiffened elk hides, which could repel arrows.

As the cold weather came on, the men added leggings, blankets, fur caps (with the ears of the animal left on) and moccasins with the fur on the inside and stuffed with grass. They also made sleeves of fox pelts. Women added fur and deerskin shirts, and blankets. There was also a form of rain gear made of woven mats.

Housing and Villages

The Takelma winter houses were rectangular lodges with plank siding and sunken floors. The dimensions were approximately 12 feet wide by up to 20 feet long. The distance from floor to smoke hole in the ceiling was thought to be six or seven feet. (Bondinell 1979) Split planks were of sugar pine (Lowlanders) or bark slabs (Uplanders). A rectangular doorway was left about three feet off the ground. A dirt ramp was constructed up to this entrance outside, and inside, a pole with steps cut into it made a ladder to the floor, which may have been two feet below ground level. Beds were woven mats, and there was enough room for storage baskets and racks overhead to dry meat. The summer homes were usually simple brush shelters around a fire pit.

Every village had at least one permanent "for men only" sweathouse, the most important structure because of religious and health reasons. This sweathouse was constructed the same as the homes except it tended to be subterranean with an earthen roof. The women's sweathouse was a small temporary lean-to of sticks and woven mats, holding about two or three persons. Women "doctors" were allowed to use the men's sweathouse though.

The villages were described as insignificant and there is no definite information available about their arrangement or size. They usually consisted of two or three families, but one account mentioned the bands to be from 30 to 150 people. The permanent

Author's interpretation of Takelma winter house.

winter villages were located at the lower elevations and near creeks and rivers, especially at the confluences of the creeks with the Rogue River. Peter Skene Ogden mentioned an uncharacteristically large village near Gold Hill which was an important center during fishing season.

Small groups travelled more easily during the summer, as they had to follow the natural harvest to higher altitudes.

For a rough estimate of the Takelma population, there were thought to be 1,154 living in 17 villages in 1852. (Bondinell 1979)

Society

The village hierarchy was by wealth and family associations. The Takelma placed a high priority on worldly goods, such as flints and dentalia, but evidently valued wealth for the favors and privileges they could do for family and friends. (Heckert 1977) Monetary compensation was required for most grievances. The chief, or more accurately, headman (da-anak), acted as the advisor-guardian, and if the group were large enough, there were sub-chiefs. The title was not necessarily inherited.

Marriages were usually pre-arranged while the bride and groom were children, and their social standing was determined by the price paid for the girl by the boy's father.

Ceremonies are but sketchily known, but include a first menses dance (puberty ritual) for girls, a feast to use up foodstuffs before moving a camp, an acorn rite performed by the men to appease the "Acorn Woman," and a first salmon rite. For this salmon ritual, an old man of the village got to sit upon the "Story Chair," which is thought to have been a big bluish rock, with a groove to hold a dip net pole, located somewhere around Rock Point, near Gold Hill. The old man would catch the first salmon of the season and tell a story of the origin of the fishing place.

Ogden and others witnessed Takelma dances. They observed "good time" dances and war dances. (Beckham 1971)

The Takelmas did not use a drum in their music, but played a flute made from a wild parsnip reed and the girls used deerhorn rattles during their ceremonies.

The bands sometimes got together to play "shinny" (a type of field hockey), to gamble, and to trade goods.

Religion

The Takelmas were a spiritual and very superstitious people. While they recognized a supreme being from the dawn of time, called Children Maker, they did not perform any services to him. Instead they recited charms and incantations to the various spirit-beings inhabiting the animals and birds, rocks, trees, and mountains. They would leave offerings of food and objects at Medicine Rock, thought to be in Lowland territory near Sexton Mountain, and at other specific locations where "spirits" lived. They had myths about imaginary beings, such as dwarfs, mermaids who tried to make canoe men overturn in the river, and rolling skulls that cry and kill all in their path. They also had a way of asking advice of or "reading" one's own excrement. (Sapir 1909)

Men or women who manifested a "guardian spirit" became shamans or Goyos, and they were treated with mixed emotion by their people because they could bring good or evil. An illness was thought to be a spirit in the form of a material object lodged somewhere in the body. A shaman was called to find and "remove" this "object." By sleight-of-hand and with great drama, they would produce it: a wood splinter or dead snake! Sometimes they actually drew blood. (Sapir 1909) The patient would then feel better and recover. There was another form of medicine person in the village, called S-omloholxa. This person was not able to cause evil, and could be called upon to counteract the work of the Goyo. Because of this, they competed with each other. The S-omloholxa also had the ability to dream of the past and the future. Their medicine seemed to be "massage therapy"—curing by rubbing the afflicted part.

Favorite characters in their stories were Coyote the trickster, Daldal the Dragonfly, Panther, Grizzly, Deer and Beaver. Tom Doty, a contemporary local storyteller, points out the similarity between the Takelma Coyote and the character Wile E. Coyote of Roadrunner cartoon fame. Both get into all kinds of trouble of their own making. They get crushed, burned, and killed, only to spring back up to life whole again!

Medicine formulas were recited when certain animals were seen or certain events happened. For instance, the phases of the moon were thought to be caused by frogs and lizards eating it. Instead of "the man in the moon," the Takelmas saw a frog in the moon. (More in *Appendix A*)

Everyday Activity

Percy Booth said there was "no such thing as a lazy Rogue" and a study of their food gathering and preparation confirms that they *had* to stay busy. (Booth 1970) The natives' "four major food groups" were acorns, salmon, deer, and camas, in order of their importance. (Hannon, TRIP Guide, 1992) The women were thought to have their own favorite camas grounds, which they protected to keep the death camas from getting mixed in. They also set fires to maintain certain favorite areas, by keeping down the brush, encouraging new growth of certain plants and helping to sustain larger populations of deer and other game. Nan Hannon writes that burning was probably as casual an event for the Takelma as mowing the lawn is to people today. (TRIP Guide, 1992)

A woman's tools were her digging stick, made of mountain mahogany with a deer antler handle, her stone mortar and pestle, and her baskets, which were even used to boil water (hot rocks were added to the water in the baskets).

Early spring brought out new growth to be used as salad greens which helped balance the winter diet of dried fish, meat, and acorn mush. Spring brought the first salmon run, early berries and camas. Summer through fall meant collecting of wild fruits, nuts, seeds and acorns. Tarweed (Madia) meadows were torched to burn off the "tar," then the seeds were beaten into funnel shaped pouches. There were deer, elk, small game to hunt and another salmon run. Crawfish were caught by the boys.

Certain animals were taboo to eat: porcupine, weasel, spotted skunks, screech owls, coyotes, wolves, eagles, snakes and frogs. These were associated with supernatural spirits. (Gray 1987) While many tribes were known to eat dogs, these did not. The only crop the Takelmas cultivated was tobacco.

TAKELMA MENU

Surf and Turf
T!ak*: fresh water mussels
Xta-n*: eel
Libis*: crawfish
Pae-wi*: salmon, roasted or smoked and dried
S'ix*: venison, boiled or raw
Hunter's Surprise Stew: deer, elk, squirrel,
jackrabbit, any or all of the above

Vegetables/Fruit
Hix*: pit-roasted camas bulbs
Yana yahals*: black oak acorn, boiled mush
Leaves of miner's lettuce, shepherd's purse, or chickweed
Tubers of Lomatium: Indian celery
Lamx*: balsamroot (sunflower): roots, leaves and seeds
K-o-x*: tarweed seeds
T'gal*: sugar pine nuts
Pi-ukh*: wild plums

Berries
Loxom*: manzanita
Oregon grape
Serviceberry
Huckleberry
Blue elderberry

(Un)Baked Goods
Pine nut/manzanita berry cakes
Xlep-x*: Camas flour cakes
Tarweed flour/hazelnut cakes
Yamx*: deer fat dough balls

Hors-d'oeuvre
Tsipi-x*: prairie-fire-toasted grasshoppers
Del*: yellow jacket larvae
Sa-l*: black and white caterpillars from ash trees

*Takelma names from *Takelma Texts*, by Edward Sapir,
or *The Takelma and Their Athapascan Neighbors* by Dennis Gray.

If the young men didn't inherit their hunting tools and weapons from their fathers, then they might spend as much as a third of their lives perfecting a set of these tools. (Booth 1970) The Takelma bow was accurate up to 50 yards, and these were the only Indians in the Northwest to hold the bow horizontally across the chest, like the crossbow. (Bondinell 1979) Deer were often rounded up and guided into snares or enclosures made of woven grasses. Indian rope was a wonder! Women wove it of iris leaves, taking a year to produce 15 feet, but it strong enough to ensnare elk! (*Living with the Land*, 1990) Dogs and fire were also used to herd the deer. The deer could then be killed with clubs. In winter, the men would stalk them in deer head disguises and run them down in the snow.

Specialized arrows were used for small game and birds. Jasper was used for arrowheads, as was obsidian obtained through trade with the Shastas or Modocs.

There were several methods of fishing: dip netting at falls, or spearing after the fish had been guided into weirs or temporary dams, also hook and line fishing from canoes by torchlight at night. Frances Johnson, one of the last full-blooded Takelma of the early 1900's, remembered her father caught 300 salmon in one night at the falls on Grave Creek.

Paradise Lost: 1826–1900
The Takelmas were very territorial, keeping their language and culture resistant to outside influence. Trading was okay, but neighboring bands knew they were not to be messed with. Molly Orton, one of the last of her people, described her Upland ancestors as "short men and mean all the time...they get mad quick." (Gray 1987) They were considered to be one of the most intelligent, cunning and warlike tribes in the Territory. (Booth 1970) Peter Ogden's Shasta guide balked at entering the Bear Creek Valley because of "the next ones."

But Ogden's discovery of the Rogue Valley completed the link between the Columbia River and the Klamath River. This corridor became the Oregon-California Trail and the two cultures, Indian and Anglo, were doomed to clash early on.

One incident of inconsistent white behavior did not improve the Takelmas' attitude toward the new people coming through the valley. A party of men left Monterey in 1834 to colonize Oregon. It was led by adventurer Ewing Young but organized by an idealist schoolteacher, Hall J. Kelly. Along the way, a group of rowdy horse-rustlers joined their group as extra hands. These men plundered an Indian village while passing through the Sacramento Valley, raping the women and killing the chief. Later, Young felt he had to kill other uninvolved Indians to keep his group from being discovered. Reaching the Bear Creek Valley, they killed and hid two Takelmas to keep the band from knowing party members were weakened by malaria.

Unfortunately, it was the next train of immigrants which was ambushed, after the bodies had been found. The Takelma realized their advantage of controlling river crossings and narrow passages.

In 1846, Jesse and Lindsay Applegate opened an alternative route to the Oregon Trail, called the Southern Emigrant Route or Applegate Trail. It came over the Green Springs Pass, now Highway 66, and meant more traffic for the Rogue Valley.

In 1848, Oregon became a territory of the United States. Until this time, the Rogue Valley had served primarily as a rest area for travelers heading for California or the Willamette Valley. Two incentives occurred in 1849–52 that caused settlers to stay in the area: the Donation Land Act of 1850, and discovery of gold on Jackson Creek and the Rogue River. The Land Act gave 320 acres of land to any adult male over 18 who had occupied his claim for four years, and included an additional 320 acres if he was married. The Land Act was valid for five years, and the population of the Oregon territory increased from 1,300 settlers in 1848, to 35,000 in 1853!

Joseph Lane, the territorial governor, tried to convince the United States government to buy the Indians' right to the land. But early on, it was thought best to remove Indians entirely from the settlements, one way or another.

Gold fever first drew groups of men to the Yreka area—Shasta country. Battles began to escalate between the miners and the Indians. Without "law and order" close by in the form of the military, the white men formed their own bands called Volunteers, who would "investigate" every instance of "Indian trouble." It is mentioned that "the acts of the Volunteers far exceeded the hostilities of the Indians...." (Beckham 1971)

Indian Wars of 1851, 1853, and 1855-56

By 1850, the Shastas and Takelmas contested every expedition through their territory, stealing and killing livestock and pack animals. In the early summer of 1850, the Indians made off with several pouches of gold dust. The miners appealed to Governor Lane, who traveled to the area and mediated a conference with the Indians. The headman tried to jump the Governor, but Lane's interpreter intervened. This chief, Aps-er-ka-har, was kept as a prisoner for two days, until another conference was scheduled. Governor Lane made an agreement with the Takelma at that time, promising an agent for the valley and gifts for every year the band kept the peace. Some stolen property was recovered, but the Indians said they had poured the gold back in the water, not realizing its value. Aps-er-ka-har, impressed with Governor Lane' conduct and fairness at this meeting, asked if he could take his name as his own. Lane allowed him to use the first syllable of his first name, Jo. He also was asked to name the Indian's wife (Sally), and two teenaged children (Ben and Mary). Governor Lane then resigned his post and headed for the gold fields of California!

In June of 1851, U.S. Army troops led by Major Philip Kearny charged into the Rogue Valley. They were simply a surveying expedition, trying to map out the Oregon-California Trail, when citizens forwarded a petition asking them to clear the road ahead of hostile Indians. Kearny hoped to surprise the Takelma at their fisheries near Lower Table Rock, but signal fires had announced their arrival. Three men were wounded, but Captain Jimmy Stuart died, becoming the first soldier killed in Indian warfare west of the Cascades. (O'Harra, *Table Rock Sentinel*, 1991) He was buried beside Bear Creek in the Phoenix area. The Army's encampment there was named Camp Stuart in his honor, as was Bear Creek briefly called Stuart

Creek. Meanwhile, Major Kearny sent for Volunteers from Yreka. Joseph Lane heard of the trouble and raised a small Volunteer army himself. The Battle of Table Rock began, spanning 10 days. Thirty Indian women and children were held as prisoners. Governor Gaines came to the Rogue Valley to renew the Indians' 1850 promise to end hostilities.

In the spring of 1852, gold was found on Jackson Creek and Jacksonville became a boomtown. Settlers there formed their own Volunteer militia. The Indians could come into Jacksonville however, and were invited into a few homes for dinner. Some of the Indians worked as servants, and a few whites adopted orphan Indian children.

Around this time, the individual names of the prominent Takelma were recorded. The headmen of the Table Rock bands were Aps-er-ka-har (Horse Rider) or Jo, and his brother, To-qua-he-ar (Wealthy) or Sam. They were considered the peace chief and the war chief, respectively. Sam's village was in the valley that now bears his name. Apparent sub-chiefs were Te-wah-hait or Elijah, and Te-cum-tum (Elk Killer) or John, possibly a son of To-qua-he-ar, whose camp was on Deer Creek. Ana-cha-arah, or Jim, and his cousin Qua-chis or Jake, led Butte Creek groups. Limpy was the leader of an Illinois River village, and his nickname evidently reflected a handicap. A village on the Rogue River below Vannoy Ferry (one of the first white settlements, now present-day Grants Pass) was led by Cho-cul-tah or George. Of the other tribes, Hart-tish, another "John," led the Applegate band and Taylor was the head of a Galice Creek band. Some Shasta leaders who appeared in the Rogue Valley were the violent Tipsu Tyee, and his sub-chiefs Sambo and Sullix.

Things began to get out of hand again following the hard winter of 1852-53. The Takelmas' way of life had been disturbed so much that it was difficult for them to secure adequate food. Farmers had plowed up their camas fields, and miners muddied the creeks. Suffering and restless, the Indians were storing up guns and ammunition, ransacking garbage piles for lead containers that tea was packed in. It was rumored that the warriors were selling or renting their women to obtain horses and guns. (Walling 1884)

After some of their men began spending an unusual amount of gold in town, members of the Indian bands along Galice and Grave Creek were rounded up and shot by Applegate miners. The old headman Taylor was hanged. They were presumed guilty of the murder of a mining party during the winter. This seemed to trigger retaliations again. After a deal involving the sale of an Indian woman fell through, the Shastas began murdering isolated men living in the hills. A killing just outside Jacksonville caused the valley settlers to become extremely nervous. In August of 1853, the paranoia became overwhelming. The Jacksonville Volunteers rounded up as many Indians as they could, including a boy, and hung them from the oak trees that lined the streets. The Table Rock bands lost approximately 14, most of whom had been hired servants. (Bondinell 1979) The Rogues attacked the tiny community of Willow Springs, killing two and burning the cabins. A wagon train on the Applegate Trail was hit while its passengers slept. A trading post full of miners was besieged on the Applegate River. The various

Volunteer companies were also on the rampage. An appeal for help went out to the nearest military outpost, Fort Jones, California, and troops hurried north to Camp Stuart. Joseph Lane, as general, was commander of the forces.

Sam's warriors were discovered in the Evans Creek area. A battle ensued that lasted around six weeks and ended up on 4,000-foot Battle Mountain, with the Indians surrendering for peace. The tired warriors, both white and Indian, had to march back to the Table Rock area from the battlefield off West Evans Creek, some twenty miles north. The Indians helped bring water and carry the wounded on litters. Lane had been shot in the shoulder, but he still retained command. A week of preparation for treaty talks went on at Camp Alden, across the river from Lower Table Rock. On September 10, 1853, eleven unarmed men rode up to the base of Lower Table Rock and hiked the steep terrain to a bench just below the cliffs. There, Joseph Lane and his troops negotiated with Jo and his men. The headmen signed a treaty, relinquishing 2,500 square miles of the upper Rogue River valley for $60,000, and establishing a reservation on and around the Table Rocks. (See *Appendixes B* and *D*)

Unfortunately, one Indian band remained particularly hostile, a group of Shastas led by Tipsu Tyee. Lane met with him in the mountains and got him to sign a treaty (that was never ratified), but Tipsu resented the others' "giving in" and continued to retaliate, murder, and stir up additional bands of Indians.

❦   ❦   ❦

"Appropriately named Fort Lane, it was commodiously and even handsomely built, and in a manner well adapted to the uses of such a post. A stockade enclosed quite a spacious area in which was a parade ground, together with barracks for private soldiers, houses for officers, an armory, a hospital, and other necessary buildings, all built of logs....A quarter of a century has seen the old fort fall into ruins, and to-day scarcely a vestige of what was once a lively encampment remains." —Walling's *History of Southern Oregon* 1884

❦   ❦   ❦

Remains of Fort Lane, DAR Monument.

In late September 1853, Fort Lane was constructed on the site of Camp Alden. It became obvious to settler and Indian alike that a constant military presence was necessary. One hundred men were assigned there. The next year was relatively quiet, but killings were still committed in the hills by unscrupulous white men and violent non-treaty Indians. On the reservation, one-fifth of the people had died or were dying from disease or starvation. Provisions of blankets and flour made in the treaty were slow in coming. Indian Agent Samuel Colver lived amongst them and sent word that he could not prevent some from going off the reservation in search of food. He noted, "They show the best possible disposition and I think with prudent management there is no chance of another war." (Robison 1943) Agent Colver also wrote: "If the powers that be in Washington knew how much good prompt action would accomplish for this valley they certainly would favor us with it." (Robison 1943)

Chief Jo died of tuberculosis in November of 1854. He had been cared for by the family of Nathaniel Dean, one of the first settlers of Willow Springs. (Bondinell 1979)

The Final Uprising 1855–56

In October of 1855, a group of Volunteers from Yreka rode into Jacksonville, knowing that the court was in session there. They had tales of an ambush in the Siskiyous, and they held a public meeting to discuss the final "extermination" of the Indians. One man, John Beeson, stood up to say it was not the Christian thing to do. Because he was known as an "Indian sympathizer," increasing threats on his life caused him to leave town in the middle of the night.

The Volunteers struck Jake's village on Butte Creek just before dawn, killing 8 men, 15 women and children. The Indians on the reservation divided. The bands under the new headman, Elijah, and Sam sought refuge at Fort Lane. The others, under Chief John, killed agency employee William Guin and went on a rampage down the valley heading for the coast. Settlers were unaware of the Indian massacre, and were caught unprepared. The Indians besieged the home of Jacob B. Wagner and burned it down around his wife and daughter. (Mr. Wagner had been escorting a temperance lecturer on her way to Crescent City and returned to find the massacre underway.)

The Indians then headed for the ranch of George Harris. He was shot as he ran into his cabin, as was his 11-year-old daughter, Sophie. Dying, he taught his wife, Mary, how to use his guns, and she managed to hold the Rogues off for around 18 hours. The Indians killed Harris' hired man, Frank Reed, and torched the outbuildings. Young David Harris, trapped outside, was never found. The Army troops were not able to arrive until the next morning, when they found Mary and Sophie hiding in the woods.

Meanwhile, people poured into Jacksonville for refuge as the horror stories filtered in. Camp Stuart became Volunteer headquarters and was described as mass confusion. Leaders managed to form the 500 men into nine companies. After a surveying party accidentally stumbled upon the location of the war party and lived to tell about it, 250 men of both the Regulars (Army) and Volunteers headed out.

The Battle of Hungry Hill was fought on the last day of October 1855, in a divide four miles up Grave Creek from the Rogue River. It was the Army's first campaign, but the Indians were ready. The Volunteers literally jumped the gun and ran straight into a fatal barrage. The Army's orders became confused, and the men experienced their first retreat. Reportedly the Volunteers blamed the Army and vice-versa. (O'Harra 1985)

The Indians laid low into November, while the Army moved its forces down the Rogue River canyon. Once again, the Army accidentally came across the Indian stronghold encamped at a place called Little Meadows, across the river from them. Deciding to attack within the next couple of days, they commenced cutting down trees to build rafts. The Indians heard the chopping noises and opened fire. And again, the Army made a "retrograde march." (O'Harra 1985)

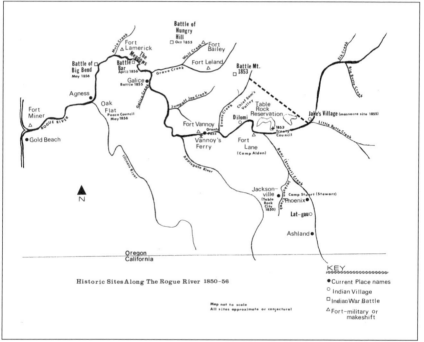

Based on maps of Walsh, Heckert and Beckham.

As another bad winter closed in, the Indians camped at Fort Lane lacked proper food, clothing, and shelter. The Indian Superintendent, Joel Palmer, was hurriedly trying to find reservation sites along the coast. (It was thought that the Oregon harbors were worthless and that the Coast Range would be a good barrier between the Indians and the settlers.) A site was finally set up, but on the edge of the Willamette Valley. It was too hard to get supplies across the coastal mountains. In the snows of January, 400 Indians left the Table Rock Reservation, marching through the mountains for the Grande Ronde Reservation. This was the beginning of "The Trail of Tears" for local Indians.

Several tribes along the Rogue River canyon were still taking out their pent-up aggressions against the pioneer settlements. Gold Beach was torched, and the Indians besieged Fort Miner. Troops were sent from as far as San Francisco to end those hostilities.

The Army finally launched a campaign to end the Indian Wars in May of 1856. A conference was set up at Oak Flat, four miles up the Illinois River from its confluence with the Rogue River. After a final battle (again caused by the Volunteers), the Indians surrendered. On June 10th, they were marched to Port Orford. Lt. Edward Ord wrote, "It almost makes me shed tears to listen to them wailing as they totter along." The Indians were then shipped aboard the steamer *Columbia* on a long and peculiar route to the Siletz Reservation, which had finally been set up along the coast.

John's band was finally captured near the end of June, and though he had sworn he would never go to the reservation, he was compelled to walk with his people the 125 miles there.

A Culture Is Lost

The Takelmas did not fit well into reservation life. The climate and food was so different on the coast than what they were accustomed to. They were weakened by the forced marches and boat rides, and were described by observers to be "wretchedly poor and destitute." The soldiers had not allowed them to bring many of their personal possessions or baskets of foodstuffs. They retained their proud and insolent attitude and took their frustration out on the other tribes gathered there, especially the native coastal tribes, some who had never fought the whites. They burned government housing and destroyed property, sometimes because of their superstitions. One of their customs was to kill the doctor if the patient died, so 100 shamans, both men and women, had been killed by 1859. Approximately 200 died the first year from the climate, poor diets, poor sanitation, fighting, lung diseases and "depression of the spirits." (Kent 1977) The official population estimate went from 590 Takelma to 385 in 1857.

Chief John and his son were sent to Alcatraz prison in San Francisco for continuing to cause unrest and rebellion on the reservation. With them gone, the Takelma lost heart. By 1865, only 121 were left.

Anthropologists visiting in the 1880's found two-thirds of the Indian people speaking English, wearing non-native clothing and living in houses. Nearly every home had a sweathouse though! Of the 14 original tribes sent to live at the Siletz reservation, some retained as few as five full-blooded members and most no more than fifty. In 1884, there were no more than 27 Takelmas. Chief John said, "It is not your wars, but your peace that kills my people."

Trying to make life easier for their children, most Indian parents discouraged them from keeping the old ways. The Indian children in the boarding school environment lost more of their customs.

When it was noticed that the Siletz reservation sat on a quarter of a million acres of timber, the government sold 75 percent of the land. In 1956, Congress terminated every tribe and band west of the Cascades. (Buan-Beckham 1991)

In 1977, the government restored the tribes to "recognized" status. The Confederated Tribes of the Siletz and Grande Ronde are the descendants of the many bands that have passed into history. While there are no known Takelma Indians living in the Rogue Valley today, one of the last Takelma headmen, George Harney, left 76 descendants scattered across the United States. George became the first chief of the Confederated Tribes of the Siletz in 1870, and he was a respected spokesman. One of his grandchildren, Agnes Taowhywee (Morningstar) Pilgrim, lives in Crescent City. She appears in a segment of a documentary, "Gifts of Our Ancestors," filmed in 1992 atop Lower Table Rock. Agnes is working hard to reclaim her heritage, remembering ironically that her mother discouraged her from learning the Takelma language in order to cope in the white world.

Agnes Taowhywee Pilgrim, Takelma descendant.

Back home in Southern Oregon, the few Rogues that remained were hunted down, although a few women were allowed to stay in the valley if they were married to white men. One was Chief Jo's daughter, Mary. Fort Lane was mothballed in 1857, and the log structure collapsed twenty five years later.

The Table Rock Community

Farming activity picked up as more settlers arrived, and the mining activity and Indian Wars died down. The staple crops were corn, wheat, rye, oats, barley, potatoes and hay, and the chief source of meat was pork, although sheep were also kept for their wool.

One of the first Donation Land Claims (DLC) in the whole valley went to Alonzo Skinner, the Indian Agent for the region, and was located southeast of Lower Table Rock, on Bear Creek. It then became the Wrisley property. Nine other men filed for DLC's in the Table Rock area, but only four appear often in records of Jackson County: William S. Bybee, William Wilson, John B. Wrisley, and Chauncey Nye. (Leavitt 1968)

Mr. Bybee was a shrewd Kentuckian who arrived in 1854 and established himself as the largest landowner in the county. He operated a ferry across the Rogue at the place where the bridge now bears his name. The first bridge was built in the late 1880's, the second in 1913 and a third in 1950.

Chauncey Nye and his brother worked gold mines in the Jacksonville area and took part in the Indian Wars. Chauncey's DLC was in the Upper

Table Rock area. Because of possible Indian retaliation, his cabin had a "palisade" surrounding it with slots for gun barrels.

John B. Wrisley arrived in 1852, and his eldest daughter, later Alice Goddard, was one of the first pioneer children born in the Rogue Valley. He eventually had 10 children. His property became the Red Skin Orchard.

William Wilson arrived from Tennessee and took out his claim near the foot of Lower Table Rock in 1852. It was supposedly on the site of an Indian graveyard. Mr. Wilson was acquainted with Chiefs Sam and Jo, and his family remembered being kept awake at night by Indian gatherings on an island in the Rogue River across from their home. Mr. Wilson had a log "fort" on his property which came in handy during the Indian Wars. Evidently, an Indian boy whom the neighboring Wrisley family had befriended, tipped them off to a planned attack, telling them, "In one more moon, the Indians are coming to kill the whites." All the neighbors then holed up at the Wilson fort. (Leavitt 1968)

While Jacksonville was known as Table Rock City from around 1850-53, the area from Bybee Bridge to Lower Table Rock was the distinct Table Rock community. There was a post office located there as early as 1872 (discontinued in 1874, reestablished in 1884, then discontinued in 1895). The community name was briefly changed to one word, Tablerock.

In March of 1879, Table Rock began School District #44. James W. Collins, who had 10 children, donated a corner of his property and his mother's house to be the first school.

Fred Hansen and his family of four children arrived in 1883. He donated an acre of land for the new schoolhouse which was built in 1892. Still standing, the old schoolhouse is now the Table Rock Bible Church.

SOHS#13990

Early homestead.

The Table Rock Bible Church, former 1892 schoolhouse.

Table Rock Championship Baseball Team. Date Unrecorded. *Front Row:* Albert Kilburn, John Nealon, Ed Vincent, Verne Pendleton. *Back Row:* Earl May, Darwin Phillips, Clark Collins, Stanley Lydiard, Carl Beebe, Lawrence Fitzpatrick.

The Stephen M. Nealons arrived in 1883 and purchased the Collins farm. Mr. Nealon had been a Union soldier in the Civil War, and he had married the daughter of a former Southern slave owner. They had 10 children, six of their daughters taught school in the Rogue Valley. May Nealon received the first diploma (eighth grade) in 1908. She then passed the teacher's exam and was ready to teach school herself. Stephen was postmaster from 1885-90 and served on the state legislature in 1895. In 1983, the Nealon farm was designated an Oregon Centennial Farm, having been in the same family for 100 years.

Other pioneer families of the area include the Pickney and Cyrus Pickens', Dr. A.C. Stanley's, R.E. Drum's and Benton Vincent's.

Regarding the summits of the Rocks, a Charlie Pankey tried to homestead the top of Lower Table Rock in the late 1800's to early 1900's, but he bailed out due to lack of water. Pankey built the first road up there, dug a well and attempted to grow corn. (Kranz and Richter 1980)

From approximately 1888 to 1910, there was an epidemic of a malaria-type illness which the settlers called ague and which caused at least one family to pack up and move.

The first telephones arrived in 1908, and the Table Rock Mutual Telephone Company came into being. The residents were stockholders, and every year, one of them was voted to be lineman, receiving a long pole to straighten out the wires after a storm.

In 1910, the Hauptmans arrived and built the store at the curve of the intersection of Table Rock and Modoc Roads.

This was also the year of the "Pear Rush." New money flowed into the valley as people were willing to pay "fabulous" prices for "pear land." (Leavitt 1968) As large orchards sprang up, raising pears became Table Rock's leading industry. Eighteen hundred acres were bought from Mr. Bybee by the Potter Palmers of Chicago. This land became the Modoc Orchard, and at a later time was owned by Harry and David. Elmer Hull helped plant the first trees and worked there for 23 years, becoming the foreman. He purchased his own orchard in 1940, the 86-acre Red Skin Orchard, considered one of the finest in the valley. He later bought up the Schaefer and Tuttle Orchards, for a total of 200 acres. The Hull orchard label was titled the Famous Table Rock Brand, and depicts the cliffs towering above an orchard in full bloom.

During World War I, every available person was needed to harvest the pears, and for the first time, women were hired, to perform their "patriotic duty."

During World War II, there was an Aircraft Observation Post on the Tuttle and Nealon properties to keep track of all planes passing over the area. Camp White, located in the present White City, literally "impacted" the area at this time. Bunkers from the artillery range can still be seen off of Antioch Road, below Upper Table Rock. Stories abound of residents finding live ammunition rounds sticking out of the dirt around the flanks of Upper Rock. (Kramer 1992)

Cars opened the community up, and in 1948, the Table Rock, Agate, Willow Springs, Tolo, Sam's Valley, and Gold Hill school districts became consolidated with that of Central Point. Table Rock maintained a primary school until 1953, however.

John Day owned the land around Lower Table Rock as well as a portion of the summit, from around 1940 to 1978. He was a famous local character, an avid sportsman and adventurer. He constructed 50 miles of jeep roads on his property, and had quite a remarkable ranch, the 4,000-acre Gold Rey Buffalo Ranch. (Ray, *Table Rock Sentinel*, Mar/Apr 1990) In addition to raising cattle and buffalo, Day added other exotic animals: yak, llamas, cheetahs, white fallow deer, and wild Russian boar. He cleared the central valley between the east and west arms of Lower Rock for additional grazing land and seeded the summit and bowl of Lower with grass and wildflower seeds. He also built the airstrip in the early 50's. (Kranz and Richter 1980)

Awakening of Preservation Interest

In 1973, the Land Conservation and Development Commission (LCDC) was created by the State Legislature. Citizens and organizations were encouraged to participate as each city and county developed comprehensive land use plans. It was noticed that the Table Rocks were unprotected from development. At that time, there were plans for a subdivision, the size of Ashland, to be built in the bowl of Lower Table Rock. (Table Rock & Kelly Slough Study Committee Minutes, 1973) Kelly Slough was in danger of becoming a gravel pit, and its cottonwoods were attractive to the logging industry.

The Table Rock and Kelly Slough Study Committee was formed, coordinated by Bill Meyer of the Sierra Club. Representatives of federal, state, county and city agencies and of local conservation groups, such as the Audubon Society and the Sierra Club, were invited to the first meeting on November 29, 1973. A Steering Committee was formed to develop goals and a plan. Some of their goals were to try to "keep the tops of Table Rock 'as is' and in public ownership, and guarantee public access to Table Rocks and Kelly Slough." (Table Rock & Kelly Slough Study Committee Minutes, 1973)

The initial response from the State Parks Department and The Nature Conservancy was lukewarm; while both encouraged the preservation efforts, neither group could commit any financial backing at that time. It seems that a guided tour of the Rocks in April of 1974 so impressed Wayne Rifer, then Coordinator of The Nature Conservancy Oregon Natural Areas Inventory, that he gave Lower Table Rock top priority.

The Bureau of Land Management already owned around 160 acres of the summit of Lower Table Rock, and the Nature Conservancy hoped to have a cooperative nature preserve. In December of 1978, The Nature Conservancy launched a public campaign, its largest fund-raising project at that time. The 2,750-acre preserve cost $500,000. As the first payment of $114,000 was due in January 1979, the money was borrowed from the Elmer Feldenheimer Land Preservation Fund. Mr. Feldenheimer had an orchard near Lower Table Rock, and he had loved to hike in the area. After Feldenheimer's death, his sister set up a revolving fund to help with Northwest conservation projects. (This fund allowed transactions to be made while the opportunity existed, and then the debt was to be repaid as soon as possible.) The Nature Conservancy received Carpenter Foundation and Cheney Foundation grants, as well as many individual donations, and the goal was reached.

In April of 1980, a plaque was placed on the lip of Lower's cliff and dedicated to the memory of Elmer Feldenheimer. (See *Appendix C*.)

Unfortunately, it was stolen from that site, but a new one has since been placed at the trailhead.

George and Hendrika Neary bought the Day ranch in the late 1970's. The Nature Conservancy sought and purchased a conservation easement from them for the 900 acres between Kelly Slough and the plateau. Jackson County later purchased Kelly Slough from the Conservancy as a future part of the Bear Creek Greenway.

Access to the top of Lower Table Rock remained a problem for several years, especially for the local landowners. At one point, the trail crossed a pig farm. In 1982, another easement was negotiated by The Nature Conservancy with property owner Brenda Greb, so that a new trail access and parking lot could be built. The first 400 feet of trail were constructed by Central Point Boy Scout Troop 40, led by Sam Fagone, and the rest of the trail was built by the State Forestry Department's Hot Shot crew. John Ifft, of the BLM, and Professors Don Mitchell and Frank Lang of the SOSC Biology Department helped design and build the trail. The Cheney Foundation donated $10,000 for fencing, signs, and parking lot construction. The trail was dedicated in April 1983 and received a write-up in *Sunset* magazine.

Meanwhile, The Bureau of Land Management nominated Upper Table Rock as an Area of Critical Environmental Concern (ACEC) in 1981. It was thus designated in 1984. Its foot trail was built by the Young Adult Conservation Corps in 1981. A new parking lot was added in 1991.

A Stewardship Committee, consisting of community members, biologists, teachers and representatives of the BLM and The Nature Conservancy, meets to help manage and make decisions regarding the Table Rock Preserve. Lower Table Rock is included in the national program, Watchable Wildlife, and interpretive signs have been installed along the trail.

Despite protests, Pacific Power's new 500 kV power line crosses between Lower and Upper Table Rocks on its way from Eugene to Medford.

Pinnacles of Lower Table Rock.

GEOLOGY

The Mystery of the Table Rocks
By David L. Kennedy

There is a dense, looming mystery in our midst that scientists have been puzzling over for decades. Just off I-5 north of Central Point are the Table Rocks. The name is no mystery: what better label for two flat-topped mountains? The question is just how did these mesas get that way, especially when the mountains all around are peaked?

The day after this fall's first drenching rain BLM Geologist Gerry Capps headed for Upper Table Rock. "There's the place where we got the samples," he says, pointing to a road cut as we neared the parking lot. Capps recently sent the rock samples to Dr. Bob Duncan at Oregon State University, who then used the potassium-argon technique to date them at 9.6 million years old.

Thus, about ten million years ago, the theory goes, a fissure opened up somewhere in the Butte Falls area and poured forth a massive lava flow that eventually cooled into basalt, what is now the 100-foot thick cap of the Table Rocks.

There's only one problem with this theory. "Volcanism ended in the Western Cascades about 17 million years ago," says Dr. Monty Elliot of the SOSC Geology Department. "The oldest dated flows in the High Cascades (cones like Mt. Hood, Mt. McLaughlin, and Mt. Shasta) are only 4.5 million years." The 9.6 million year date lands smack in between them. "That's why I've expressed skepticism about that date," says Elliot.

With the top of Upper Table Rock shrouded in fog, Capps and I started up the trail. Within ten yards a huge donut of gummy clay clung to each boot, forcing us into a curious waddle. This "gumbo" ("Which you never walk on in the fall after a rain," Capps jokes) is the result of erosion from nearby ancient volcanoes.

Erosion is a constant process, says Capps. It is how the Table Rocks came to rise 800 feet above the Rogue River, which today winds past their feet. Underlying the valley from White City to Jacksonville and up Bear Creek is a layer of sandstone and gravel called the Payne Cliff Formation, named after the imposing cliffs off Fern Valley Road north of Phoenix. This sandstone was deposited between 66 and 37 million years ago, according to Elliot, from streams tumbling out of the surrounding mountains. It once filled the valley to the height of the Table Rocks and Ashland—about 2,000 feet.

Elliot says the lava flowed over this layer in a massive sheet. The sandstone, being softer than the basalt lava, eroded around the Table Rocks, leaving them high and dry. "One of the reasons the Table Rocks are still standing after all these millions of years is that after it rains they dry out quickly, so chemical erosion has less effect," he says, "Wind erosion is grossly over-rated."

Capps believes that rather than covering everything, the hot lava just poured down an ancient river canyon, turning the water to steam as it went. This would account for the sinuous shape of the Table Rocks, he says. "You'd see big basalt boulders strewn all around the valley floor" if the lava had covered the whole area, says Capps.

Elliott maintains the boulders eroded away because they were buried in moist soil. "The Rogue Valley was not covered by an ice sheet during the Ice Age," he says, "but it was a lot colder and wetter."

"One of the few places you can see the base of the flow," says Capps, are the caves beneath Upper Table Rock. (Capps warns that the caves are dangerous and the bats should not be disturbed.) "The caves have really left some questions. If it flowed over a river there'd be river gravels under the cap," he says. They haven't found river gravels yet.

The caves were dug by miners. "An old fella came into the BLM with a vial of gold once," says Capps, "He said he got it in an old mine shaft under the Table Rocks." If that's true, speculates Capps, the presence of gold strongly suggests gold's companion, river gravels.

Jim Smith of the U.S. Geological Survey, who has done extensive research on the southern Oregon Cascades, says, "There's no doubt in my mind it (the lava) flowed down an old drainage system." The question remains about whether the lava came from the Western or High Cascades.

"The Western Cascades near Medford...tip eastward up to 30 degrees," says Smith. "What I call the Western Cascades is this tipping rock. The Table Rocks don't tip to the east but they were one of the first volcanic units to be deposited on this tipping sequence," he says. "It is a very large volume of material."

This suggests the origin of the Table Rocks is in the early High Cascades. Elliot says the High Cascades "could be older (than 4.5 million years) perhaps underneath where they haven't been dated." If the 9.6 million year date is correct it could represent the oldest lava of the High Cascades.

The tremendous vistas from the top of the Rocks took our breath away. We walked across the hard surface where Capps kicked the ground and took up a handful of soil. "Basalt typically erodes to clay, but the soil on top is crumbly, not clayey," he says. "You'd think after ten million years there'd be more soil on top, wouldn't you?"

Out near Table Rock the wind careens across the valley floor and strikes the vertical cliffs of Upper Table Rock. There it whooshes upward and tousles Capps' hair as he stands at the top of the cliff. "I don't think by any stretch of the imagination we really know how it (Table Rock) was formed," he says. "There's too much rock missing." There are tough questions that no one is going to answer right away. But it means we can all think freely about them as we climb the trail, putting ourselves between the Table Rocks, and a hard place.

Originally appeared in the *Ashland Gazette*, November 1992. Reprinted with permission by the author.

Table Rock Geologic Field Guide
by Gerard Capps

ILLUSTRATIONS BY DEE DUNCAN

This field guide is designed to help you understand the geologic processes that created a prominent landmark of Southern Oregon. The Table Rocks stand out in contrast to the surrounding rolling hills of the Rogue Valley by their sheer vertical cliff faces and nearly horizontal flat tops. Mesas like these are more common in the volcanic terrain of Eastern Oregon. There are no other similar mesas in western Oregon. Most of the geologic features you will observe are found on both the Upper and Lower Table Rocks; however, this guide is designed for hiking the trail on Upper Table Rock.

On this hike you will observe two distinct rock types. The lower 700 feet of Table Rocks is sandstone of the Payne Cliff Formation and the upper 120+ feet is *basalt* cap rock. (See *Glossary,* page 45, for italicized words.)

From the trailhead on Modoc Road, you ascend approximately 800 feet to the top of Table Rock. For the first 700 feet in elevation you will observe a tan sandy rock formation known as the Payne Cliff Formation. This sandstone underlies most of the

Gerry Capps heads up a Saturday field trip, Upper Table Rock.

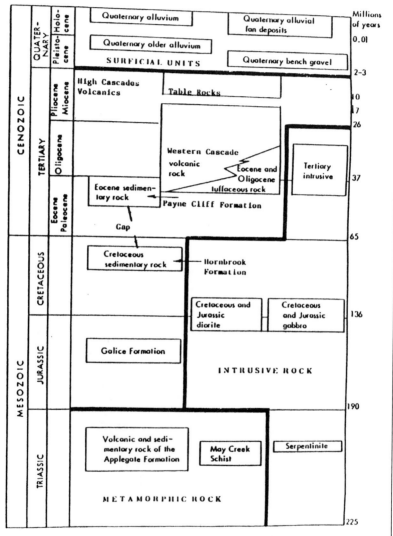

Adapted From:

LAND USE GEOLOGY OF CENTRAL JACKSON COUNTY

Time distribution of geologic units.

Geologic Time Chart.

Rogue Valley from Ashland to Sams Valley. The lower portion of this formation contains river-deposited *conglomerates* derived from erosion of a Klamath *metamorphic* terrain from the south. Progressing upward in the formation, the rocks grade into sandstone and siltstone interbedded with mudstone. The upper portion of the Payne Cliff Formation contains the first rock fragments of volcanic origin.

Also included within the Payne Cliff rocks are coal seams, *Upper Eocene* fossil leaves and carbonized tree trunks.

If you were to walk this trail during the winter or wetter periods of the year, you would find the trail slippery and sticky because the volcanic sediments in the upper Payne Cliff Formation weather to what is commonly called gumbo clay (a clay that expands when wet). Conversely the clay shrinks as it dries, forming cracks similar to the *columnar jointing* of Table Rock.

The fossil leaves of the Payne Cliff Formation have been identified as *Upper Eocene* (approximately 37 ± 2 million years), yet a recent dating of the overlying basalt reveals the cap rock to be 9.6 million years old (Radiometric age date, OSU). There is therefore a huge gap of 30 million years before the sandstone got its cap. (See Geologic Time Chart.)

Prior to the eruption that formed the Table Rocks, widespread volcanism began to form the Western Cascades from northern California near the Siskiyou Summit (Pilot Rock) to the Canadian border. Most of the hills on the east side of the valley are volcanic rocks of the Western Cascades. Age dates of these rocks up and down the range have determined that the oldest volcanic rocks are approximately 43 to 45 million years old and form the western flanks of the Cascades. In southern Oregon, the oldest dated rocks are about 35 million years old. Age dating of the volcanic rocks indicates volcanism gradually shifted to the east over time. Volcanism has continued throughout this interval to the present, but the volume of material erupted has declined over time.

The Western Cascade volcanoes poured out vast amounts of basalt from vents along this north-south chain, each vent building a *shield volcano*. The numerous volcanoes built upon each other with overlapping basalt and *pyroclastic* flows. In the south Cascades it is believed there was a long period of inactivity from 17 to 10 million years age with severe erosion dissecting these ancient volcanoes to the point where they are now

Sheli Parkison admires her "gumbo" footwear—January, Upper Table Rock.

unrecognizable as volcanoes. The best exposures of the Western Cascades are along the Green Springs Highway (OR 66). As you descend west from the Green Springs summit, you drive down into older rock units.

The final volcanic event began 10 million years ago with the formation of the High Cascades *andesitic composite volcanoes*. Andesite is a more viscous lava than basalt and tends to retain gases, making them more explosive. Because the rock does not flow easily, like basalt, it builds steep-sided cones. Examples include Mt. Pitt (McLoughlin), Mt. Shasta, Mt. Bachelor and all the remaining picturesque volcanoes of the Cascades.

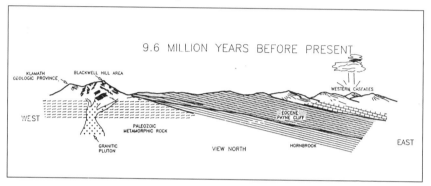

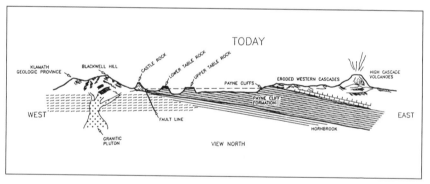

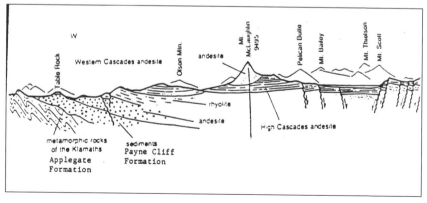

Volcanic Cross Section.

The Hike

As you ascend the slopes of the trail, you will see occasional large truck-sized boulders next to the trail. You may have noticed some of these boulders next to the road as you drove east on Modoc Road. The rock has a fracture pattern that gives the appearance of strands of rope, called *columnar jointing*. These cracks are the result of internal shrinking while the original exterior volume does not shrink as the molten basalt cooled. The boulders are derived from the collapse of a larger basalt flow than exists today. If we were to map the location of all the known boulders scattered around the valley, we might learn the original extent of the flow and its source.

You may also see rounded river gravel on the trail. These rounded gravels are probably *weathering* out of gravel beds within the Payne Cliff Formation which contains Eocene volcanic river gravels. There is also the possibility that the gravels are perched remnants of a river which has long since changed its course.

As you approach the summit, notice the rock-piles (talus). Because of the vertical jointing pattern of the Table Rocks, water seeps into these joints and expands during freezing weather, cracking the rock, which then falls on the slopes. This talus slope builds up until the unstable pile of rocks collapse, sending a wave of loose rock out onto the flat area to form the unusual patterned talus field.

Field trippers pass truck-sized boulder, Upper Table Rock.

Unfortunately this talus covers an important piece of evidence needed to understand the deposition of the Table Rock. The talus has buried the contact between the basalt flow and the underlying Payne Cliff Formation. You can, however, see this contact in one of the caves on Upper Table Rock.

(The editor has removed the section describing finding the caves. The climb may be hazardous and crosses snake habitat. It is best to take a guided hike. Also, the entrance to the trail has since been covered.)

Across a talus field, at the very base of the cliffs, are found a series of four caves. Two of the caves are formed by the fractures in the Table Rock that extend from the top to the bottom in the flow. In some cases the fractures run across the length of the flow. The fractures are up to 15 feet wide but they average eight feet. Miners have excavated rock looking for gold-bearing gravel under the flow. The two other caves were also excavated by prospectors, but these diggings were in natural cavities in the base of the basalt flow. You may observe the bottom of the black basalt overlies a sometimes porous rock and light soft granular rock. Basalt which is deposited in water develops this scoriaceous texture by incorporating the water in the rock which then forms steam bubbles. The light soft rock is the result of *weathering* processes that have altered the minerals in the rock to clay.

If you plan to go into the caves, you should carry a good flashlight and wear a hard hat. *One of the caves has a 30 foot drop into a pool of water.*

A Talus Field, from Bench Trail, Lower Table Rock.

There are three caves you can walk into, the fourth cave is just a small pit. While at the caves, notice there is a different fracture pattern near the base of the flow. The jointing has a large spacing and the rock appears fresher (less weathered). The lower portion of the flow is insulated by the ground and cools more slowly than the upper three-quarters and therefore the fractures have a larger spacing and the rock is less weathered.

Returning to the main trail, you will climb to the top of Table Rock. If you stay to the east side of the arm and walk north, you will notice the absence of significant soil. What little soil exists is granular rock fragments containing no clay. Since the rock is 9.6 million years old, it should have developed a soil profile. As you proceed north, you will find circular mounds and linear depressions filled

Geology group investigates a cave, Upper Table Rock.

with soil. These linear features are found all the way north on this arm of Table Rock and extend across the arm. These are the tension fractures that run top to bottom, cutting the flow completely.

There are several theories about why there is no soil. One is, soil that develops on Table Rock is derived by weathering of the rocks, but before the granular soil weathers to clay, it is blown like sand dunes into the numerous fractures and washed off the edge of the cliffs. There are at least two other explanations for the granular soil mounds. Some have suggested gophers have collected the soil as they search for food; another possibility is violent shaking by earthquakes built the mounds. These mounds appear to be tapered and linear for sometimes a hundred feet or more in the same direction, which suggests constant winds from the north or south may have shaped them and transported them into the fracture traps.

You must walk all the way to the west edge of this arm of Upper Table Rock and look west across Lower Table Rock to see the peak that rises about 130 feet above Lower Table Rock. This peak is a small remnant of the same basalt flow, known as Castle Rock. Assuming that the basalt flow was deposited forming a flat horizontal surface, the elevation difference must be attributed to post-deposition faulting. (See page 42, A.) Castle Rock overlies the Applegate Formation, a much older formation than the Payne Cliff Formation.

Both Upper and Lower Table Rocks have a concave, horseshoe shape facing south. This shape is unusual for eroding basalt mesas, in fact, most mesas are rather symmetrically round or linear. However, if the basalt poured down a deep river canyon, say 100 feet deep, it would follow the sinuous path of the river and assume the shape of the canyon. If the basalt

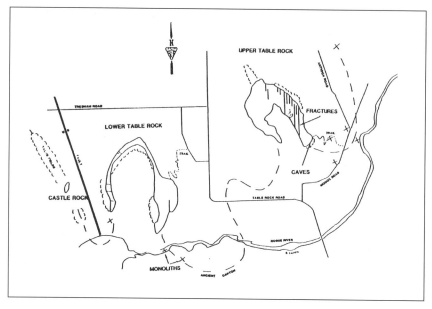

A. Basalt flow may have followed ancient river canyon.

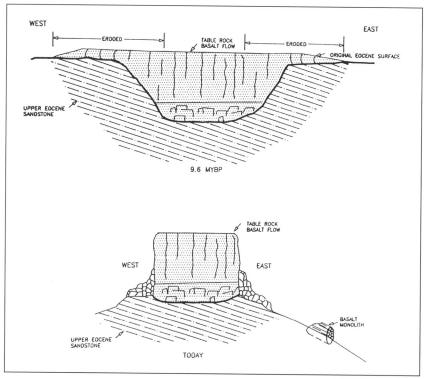

B. Process of inverted topography.

flow exceeded the capacity of the canyon, it would spill over the top with a thin veneer of basalt. The basalt, being more resistant to erosion, protected the underlying Payne Cliff sandstone while the rest of the valley slowly melted away in ten million years. This is called inverted topography. (See page 42, B.)

There are several features that support the theory that the basalt was deposited in an ancient river canyon. (See pages 46–47.)

A. The basalt "monoliths" have been plotted on the preceeding map (See page 42, A.) to show their distribution. They are located in a configuration which can be interpreted as following a sinuous path. The converse of that statement is that they are not found randomly around the valley floor and in fact their absence around the buttes and between the buttes is additional evidence that this flow did not cover a wider area.

B. The fractures of the basalt may be structurally controlled by weakness in the underlying sandstone, but aerial photos of the fracture pattern suggest that the fractures may be the result of weakness created from the sinuous path or bending of the molten lava within the meanders. (See below.)

C. The "monoliths" and some cobbles have been found 300 meters from the cliff vertical faces, but these rocks have irregular shapes that probably would prevent them from rolling very far. These isolated monoliths may be that portion of the original flow that overspilled the canyon walls, and they have not moved except vertically as the underlying sandstone eroded out from underneath. (See page 42, B.)

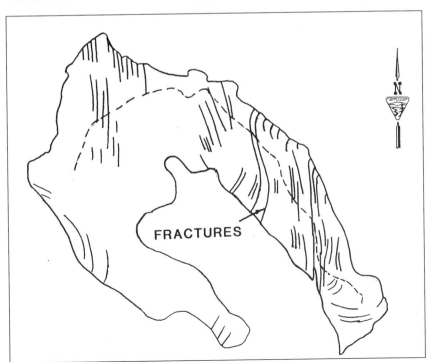

Tension fractures on Upper Table Rock.

D. There are no river gravels of any significance north of the present Rogue River except a small area near the junction of Antioch Road and Modoc Road, therefore there has not been the erosion energy needed to carve this basalt into its present shape and carry away the basalt of a much more extensive flow.

Although there are some basalt flows near Trail, Lost Creek Lake, and Prospect which resemble Table Rock, those basalt flows have age dates three million years younger than Table Rocks. During the volcanic history of the Western Cascades, numerous basalt flows poured down eroded canyons, referred to as intercanyon flows, but it would be a great leap of imagination to propose the Table Rocks are an intercanyon basalt flow that had its source in the Prospect area. *While it is physically possible for basalt to flow that far*, it is not likely that the Rogue River has maintained its present course for ten million years.

Structural Deformation of The Rocks

Upper and Lower Table Rocks are both tilted but in different directions. Upper Table Rock is tilted to the southeast about 1% and Lower Table Rock is tilted to the southwest about 1%. This may mean there is some post-deposition arching between the two slabs. This may also explain the higher elevations of the north end of Upper Table Rock.

Finally, consider where else we might find basalt flows with such prominent columnar jointing, flat as a table, and that are one mile wide and two miles long and 120+ feet thick in the Western Cascades. Almost all basalt flows in the Western Cascades are no more than 500 feet in width or length. There are exceptions, but none are anywhere the magnitude of Table Rock. Given the size of the flow and the relatively flat surrounding topography, there should be more Table Rock outcrops somewhere in the Rogue Drainage. But since there are none to be found, it may be that the Table Rock flow is a unique local feature with a local source. It may be that this flow was never much larger than its present distribution. This idea may change with further study of the outcrops found near Trail, Lost Creek Lake, and Prospect.

Summary

Recent field studies suggest the Table Rock basalt flow may have been deposited in a canyon containing water. Its horseshoe shape is the result of filling ancient canyon meanders. The size of the flow may not have been much larger than what is found today. The 9.6-million-year-old rock has been deformed by arching between Upper and Lower Table Rock. Castle Rock has been uplifted 130 feet by a fault more recent than the basalt flow that formed Table Rock. Because of the limited known rock identified as part of the Table Rocks, we cannot at this time, identify with any certainty the source of this flow.

(The source of the flow has since been located and will be revealed in a report in the journal "Oregon Geology" sometime in early 1994. *—Editor*)

Glossary

Andesite Composite Volcano: Volcano constructed by interbedded flows of lava and ash. Andesite refers to chemical composition of lava having 62% to 57% SiO2. Usually gray lava.

Basalt: An extrusive volcanic rock usually black with less than 57% SiO2. Both andesite and basalt have fine grained minerals difficult to identify. One of the identifying features of Table Rock basalt is the 1/4" laths of calcic plagioclase easily identified in hand specimens.

Columnar Jointing: Shrinkage cracks in basalt due to cooling basalt. Frequently hexagonal and perpendicular to the flow surface.

Conglomerate: A sedimentary rock composed of rounded gravel cemented together by a matrix of calcite, clay, silica, or sand.

Metamorphic: Rocks formed in response to pronounced temperature, pressure, and chemical changes. Volcanic and sedimentary rocks can by altered (metamorphosed) by increased pressure and temperature.

Pyroclastic: Explosively ejected volcanic particles.

Shield Volcano: A broad, gentle volcanic cone of domical shape, usually several tens or hundreds of square miles in area, built chiefly of overlapping basalt lava flows.

Upper Eocene: A time period when mammals as we know them appeared (36 to 43 million years before present time).

Weathering: Process which breaks down rock to soil. These include reaction to air, water, biological reaction, and physical processes.

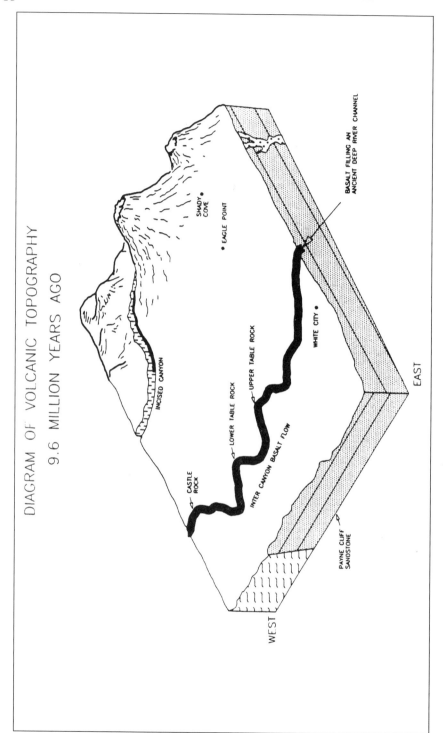

DIAGRAM OF VOLCANIC TOPOGRAPHY
9.6 MILLION YEARS AGO

INCISED CANYON

CASTLE ROCK

LOWER TABLE ROCK

UPPER TABLE ROCK

INTER CANYON BASALT FLOW

SHADY COVE

EAGLE POINT

WHITE CITY

BASALT FILLING AN ANCIENT DEEP RIVER CHANNEL

PAYNE CLIFF SANDSTONE

WEST

EAST

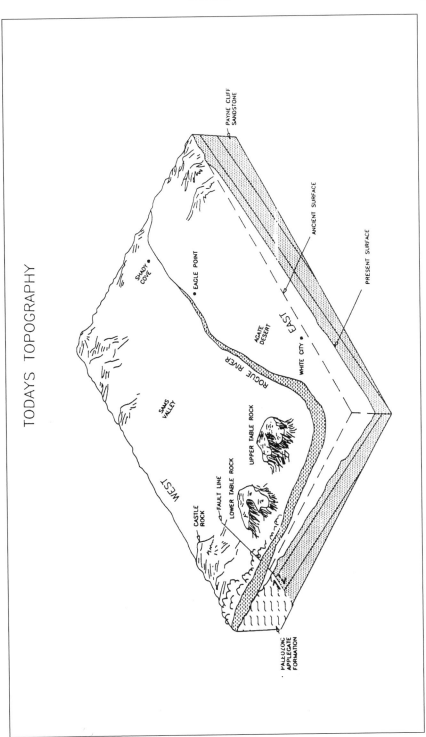

TODAYS TOPOGRAPHY

Aerial view of Lower Table Rock.

Aerial view of Upper Table Rock.

Dusky-footed wood rat den, Lower Table Rock.

FAUNA

ILLUSTRATIONS BY ALAN ST. JOHN

Luckily, the wildlife on The Rocks is not too wild! Most of us encounter only birds, lizards, frogs, and a variety of insects. This is probably because most critters are asleep while we are there, and vice-versa. Animals' nocturnal habits help them cope with the dry conditions upon the summits. There is evidence of many of these creatures if you look carefully for their signs and tracks.

Amphibians

The vernal pools on the summits teem with tadpoles from March through May. Two types of amphibians are found here, the western toad (*Bufo boreas*) and the Pacific tree frog (*Hyla regilla*). While youngsters in the pools, they are herbivorous, eating the algae in the water. After they get their lungs, it's "Look out, bugs!" It is amazing how the amphibians survive the long drought period. Studies have found that toads and gophers may exist together in burrows, and that the tree frogs also may use rodent burrows. (Bork 1978) Amphibians also have the ability to absorb water through their skins, allowing them to use the dew for moisture.

The western toad is the common garden toad, and is only rarely seen on The Rocks. If you do happen to find one and hold it, do *not* rub your eyes, because toads produce weak poisons in their skin glands that are irritating to mucous membranes. (Leviton)

Pacific tree frogs have a large population on The Rocks until around June, when they are either snuggled up in burrows or have died off. They have the distinctive, famous, loud croak. They are able to change color to match their environment, varying from green to brown, and they have a black line through their eyes. Their feet have long toes with obvious pads. While this frog is a tree dweller, I have nearly stepped on them in the scabland areas.

Reptiles

Three lizard species were found, the western fence lizard (*Sceloporus occidentalis*), the southern alligator lizard (*Gerrobonotus multicarinatus*), and the western skink (*Eumeces skiltonianus*).

The western fence lizard is the most common and usually the only one seen. Lizards are able to tolerate the daytime heat better than snakes, so the sudden scurrying heard in the dry leaves is usually just the fence lizard. The fence lizard has two rows of dark, brown to black splotches on its back and distinctive blue blotches on its throat and belly (especially vivid on the males). They can be captured in the mornings, when they are sluggish, but they get faster as the day heats up. They have the snap-off tail. Fence lizards are highly territorial and will defend their homes. This lizard has two funny habits: head-bobbing, which may either be a territorial display or for depth-perception, and avoidance of observation by going round and round a tree, staying on the opposite side from where the the an intruder is.

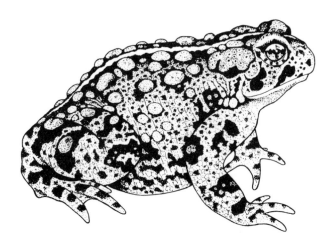

Western Toad
Bufo boreas

Pacific Tree Frog
Hyla regilla

Amphibians   *(Not to scale.)*

Western Fence Lizard
Sceloporus occidentalis

Western Skink
Eumeces skiltonianus

Southern Alligator Lizard
Gerrohonotus multicarinatus

Reptiles/Lizards   *(Not to scale.)*

They hibernate in the winter. Favorite foods include beetles, aphids, ants, wasps, and spiders.

Alligator lizards are common in the Rogue Valley but are rather difficult find on The Rocks (unless you are a child). They may be brown or a reddish, yellowish or greenish-brown, with dark crossbands on the body and tail, and may have brick red sides with white flecks. Their young have a broad tan stripe that runs down their backs. They can reach 16 inches long, most of it tail. This tail is prehensile, used like a hand when climbing, wrapping around limbs. This lizard is aggressive and will bite and hang on when captured. It eats beetles and spiders, centipedes, slugs, snails, and worms. It also will occasionally eat young mice or raid bird nests.

Western skinks, also called blue-tailed skinks, have lengthwise brown and white stripes, the young having bright blue tails which become duller in adulthood. This feature really catches one's eye amongst the browns of The Rocks, and helps the juveniles survive by causing predators to notice the tail, which when grabbed, breaks off. The female lays up to six eggs under stones, in cavities or burrows, and she stays to protect them until the young hatch, the only reptile in Oregon that does this. They are aggressive and fast. Favorite foods include insects, earthworms, spiders, and sometimes their own young.

Snakes

Western Rattlesnake	*Crotalus viridis*
Common Garter Snake	*Thamnophis sirtalis*
Western Garter Snake	*Thamnophis elegans*
Western Ringnecked Snake	*Diadophis punctatus*
Racer	*Coluber constrictor*
Striped Whipsnake	*Masticophis taeniatus*
Gopher Snake	*Pituophis melanoleucus*
California Mountain Kingsnake	*Lampropeltis zonata*
Common Kingsnake	*Lampropeltis getulus*

Only the Western Rattlesnake is poisonous. It tends to cause much apprehension after the end of April. Because these snakes give birth to live young and winter together in dens (hibernacula), it is best to avoid the talus slopes in the spring and the fall, when they may all be coming or going. Other times to be cautious are summer mornings and evenings, when they are most active. The blazing hot summer afternoons cause them usually to be well out of sight, trying to keep cool.

This is the only species of rattlesnake found in the Pacific Northwest. Rattlers are classified as pit vipers, triangular headed with deep depressions between the eyes and nostrils. The pits are heat sensors to help the snake locate its prey. These sensors detect temperature differences of less than one degree centigrade, but the effective range is only about one foot. Rattlers will not chase you, but they do not have to be coiled to strike nor will they always rattle a warning. (St. John 1980)

They tend to be beige with dark blotches and dark "eyeliner." They average two-three feet in length. The rattles on the end of their tails are made of a fingernail-like tissue that forms a new "button" every time the snake molts. Because the snake may molt several times in one year, count-ing the rattles is not an indication of its age. (St. John 1980) Molting is not a good time to run into these guys either; they are more aggressive because they can not see with their skin over their eyes! Rattlers' favorite food is rodent, but they also eat nestling birds, lizards, and toads.

The two species of garter snakes are hard to tell apart. They can also be confused with the only other snake in Oregon having lengthwise stripes, the striped whipsnake. The garters have small ridges on their scales, while the whipsnake appears smooth. The common garter is gener-ally bigger than the western. Both can get to be four feet long. If you cap-ture a garter, it may squirt a smelly musk fluid from an anal gland onto you. This is truly a skunk-like defense, and friends tell me the odor lasts for days. Garters prefer the moist grassy habitats. They bear live young, sometimes up to 50.

The ringneck snake is strikingly colored: brown back, a yellow/orange band around its neck, and a bright orangish-red belly. For defense, they have a distinctive way of coiling their tails up, showing off the bright undersides. They are not larger than twenty-two inches. They are egg-lay-ers. Rarely seen, the ringneck lives in the oak woodland, under rocks and logs, and in old rotting stumps. It eats worms, slugs, lizards, frogs, and small snakes, including its own.

Western yellow-bellied racers have a smooth, single-colored topside: tan to greenish brown, with a light yellow or faintly bluish belly. They are also called blue racers. They seem to glide along, with their heads held up. Their average length is two to three feet, but they can grow to over four feet long. They are very aggressive and will bite when handled. The grass-land and oak woodland are their favorite habitats. They are out during the day. Foods include frogs, small rodents, and other snakes. They are com-munal: they hibernate with rattlesnakes and gopher snakes and lay their eggs in with other snake and lizard eggs.

Oregon's longest snake is the striped whipsnake, sometimes reaching 6 feet. If captured, it bites and "whips" the captor's face and body with its tail. It is a close relative of the racer. They prefer dry open places but will head for the brush to escape, and they can glide over the tops of bushes at high speed. The Rogue Valley is an island for this reptile, its usual domain being the sagebrush plains and canyons east of the Cascades. (St. John 1980) It is very rarely seen here, though. Favorite foods include rodents, lizards, insects, and other snakes—even rattlers. They are out during the daytime.

The gopher snake, also known as the bull snake, is often mistaken for a rattler because of similar coloration, and its mimicking of the rattler by puffing up its neck and shaking its tail. It is active in the daytime. It favors the fields and oak woodlands. Favorite foods are the rodents, but also eats lizards and young birds. It kills its prey by constricting them. It hibernates for the winter and is an egg-layer.

The California mountain king snake has beautiful black, white, and red bands, which cause it to be called the false coral or coral king snake. Luckily, there are no true coral snakes in the Pacific Northwest, so you do not have to worry about which order the colors are in! Their average size is from two to just over three feet long. Its relative, the common king, is

Western Rattlesnake
Crotalus viridis

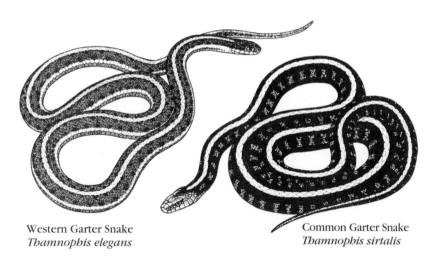

Western Garter Snake
Thamnophis elegans

Common Garter Snake
Thamnophis sirtalis

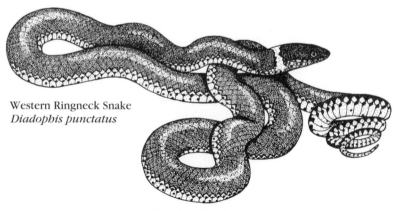

Western Ringneck Snake
Diadophis punctatus

Reptiles/Snakes

(Not to scale.)

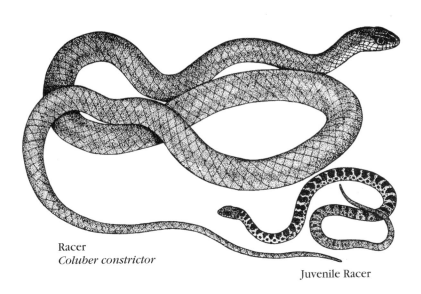

Racer
Coluber constrictor

Juvenile Racer

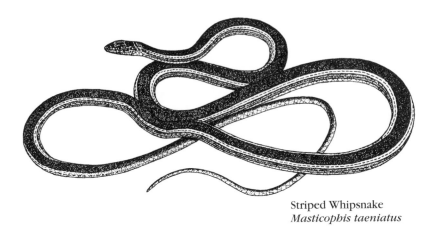

Striped Whipsnake
Masticophis taeniatus

Reptiles/Snakes

(Not to scale.)

Gopher Snake
Pituophis melanoleucus

Common Kingsnake
Lampropeltis getulus

California Mountain Kingsnake
Lampropeltis zonata

Reptiles/Snakes   *(Not to scale.)*

larger, reaching four feet or more, and is usually black with white encircling crossbands. Both of these snakes are in their northern-most range. King snakes are famous for being immune to rattlesnake venom, but they do not seek them out. In fact, when running into a king snake, the rattler may behave in completely different manner, not even bothering to assume its regular striking pose. It flattens its head and neck down and swings a loop of its body, evidently trying to distract or thrash the king snake. The kings eat all kinds of snakes, including their own, lizards, frogs, small rodents, and birds' eggs.

Some Notes About Rattlesnake Bites
Obviously, avoidance is better than treatment!

•Do not tease or handle snakes, as even dead ones can strike by reflex and inject venom several hours after death.

•Unprotected hands should not reach under logs or stones or into cracks or crevices without looking first.

•These snakes are nocturnal. Walking barefoot or collecting firewood after dark are the two most common ways to get bitten.

•Snakes rarely strike higher than the ankle, so loose fitting pants and high top hiking boots are favored.

A snake will strike out if it is cornered or, of course, stepped on. (Wouldn't you?)

There are varying opinions of what to do if you have been bitten, especially whether to walk out or be carried. The snake may have injected little, if any, venom (a comforting thought). There is general agreement of what *not* to do: no tourniquets, no ice packs, no cutting and suction.

Two good, yet differing, descriptions of snakebite first-aid are in *Medicine for Mountaineering* by James A. Wilkerson, and *The Outward Bound Wilderness First-Aid Handbook* by Jeff Isaac and Peter Goth.

Mammals
Usually the only mammals you may get to see here are the most common rodents: California ground squirrels (*Spermophilus beecheyi*), western gray squirrels (*Sciurus griseus*), and California voles (*Microtus californicus*). Hikers may notice the burrows of the ground squirrels in the banks of the trail. They often live in colonies. They aestivate, or go into a dormant state, in the late summer, and hibernate through the winter. These guys are brown with light flecks or spots, a darker triangle shaped cape across the shoulders, and less bushy tails than the gray squirrels. The ground squirrel is also a tree climber, and eats and stores seeds, acorns, berries, eggs, and insects. This squirrel can bark and whistle, but it usually chirps a warning.

Western gray squirrels are more active in the morning. Almost everyone can recognize them: they have distinctive bushy tails, silver gray coats, and white bellies. One must look 20 feet or more up a tree to see their nests, which are in cavities such as former woodpecker holes, or built of sticks and shredded bark. Their favorite food is the acorn, supplemented with conifer seeds and the cambium layer of tree trunks. They also store up food in holes. The gray squirrel has a hoarse bark.

On the summits, you may see tiny runways in the grasses, especially on the mounds, which indicates the presence of the California vole. It is small and mouse-like, with small ears, a short tail, and grayish-brown coloring with pale feet. These fellows are busy, out day and night feeding on grasses and other vegetation.

Other rodents that leave visible signs, but which themselves are rarely seen, are the valley pocket gopher (*Thomomys bottae*), and the dusky-footed wood rat (*Neotoma fuscipes*).

Those gophers work day or night, eating roots and bulbs of plants, which they stuff into external, fur-lined "pockets" in their cheeks. The gopher leaves its burrow plugged with the last of the dirt pushed to the surface, never leaving it open for long.

The dusky-footed wood rat is a member of the pack rat family. It is squirrel-sized, with its tail almost the same length as its body, and is nocturnal. Wood rats eat mostly greens, but also fruits, nuts, and seeds. They do not need water to drink, but must get it from succulent vegetation. (Bork 1978) Their presence is detected by a remarkable sign: huge pyramidal piles of branches and bark that are their dens. You can best see the wood rat "condos" from the trail on Lower Table Rock, in the madrone-black oak woodland. (I imagined someone was cleaning up the forest and sweeping the debris up into piles!) These dens can be up to four feet high, with separate bedrooms, bathrooms, and pantries. There are tunnels and trails leading to their feeding grounds or to other lodges.

The Rocks are islands to the Heerman kangaroo rat, *Dipodomys heermanni*, which lives here north of its California home range. Kangaroo rats are really bipeds, hopping on long hind feet and maneuvering with their tails. Their tracks show only hind feet and the tips of the tails. (Kritzman 1977) These rats are approximately a foot long, with a white-tipped tail. They tend to stay active all year, neither aestivating nor hibernating, but staying down in their cool moist burrows during the day. They have amazing moisture conserving mechanisms, and can exist on water produced only metabolically.

Two other chiefly nocturnal mammals have been spotted on the Table Rocks, but since they prefer habitats near sources of water, they may have been just visitors. These were the raccoon, *Procyon lotor*, and the long-tailed weasel, *Mustela frenata*. Perfectly round, open burrows on the summits may be the homes of the long-tailed weasel while the vernal pools are present.

The black-tailed jack rabbit, *Lepus californicus*, has been sighted on Upper Table Rock. Its activity periods are from early evening through early morning, avoiding the warm dry daytime. Its large ears act as radiators to dissipate heat and maintain its body temperature. (Bork 1978)

The only *big* mammal you are likely to encounter are the range cattle on Upper Table Rock. Signs of their presence include patches of mashed down vegetation, holes where hooves have sunk into the vernal pool areas and those distinctive "pies." I had been walking toward the rim one afternoon and turned to see a large black creature in the grasses about midway across the summit. Thinking it was a bear, my knees suddenly became quite weak. Then I noticed the rest of the herd standing in the shade.

Black tail deer may be seen if one is up there early enough or late enough. Deer tracks are common in the soft mud of the trails. Black bears have been known to visit the productive manzanita chaparral patches in the fall. (Borgias 1992) Coyotes are the primary predators still left on The Rocks. (Borgias 1992) They keep the rodent population nervous. It is easy to identify coyote feces or "scat" found on the summit trails. Coyote scat resembles that of a cat, and contains the fur and bones of last night's meal. Their tracks may be mistaken for those of dogs.

There are signs of bobcats, but grey wolves and mountain lions are long gone due to historic trapping and hunting. (Borgias 1992)

As for flying mammals, two species of bat were mist-netted over cattle watering ponds in the bowl of Lower Table Rock, and there are signs of them living in the caves of Upper Table Rock. (See page 34.)

Other Mammals That May Frequent The Rocks
(Modified from the charts of Kranz, Richter and Bork.)
•porcupines
•striped skunks
•deer mice, harvest mice, western red-backed mice, and pinon mice
•western moles
•vagrant shrews and Trowbridge shrews
•hoary bats, brown bats, lump-nosed bats, silver-haired bats, and pallid bats
•gray foxes and red foxes
•northern flying squirrels
•brush rabbits
•Nuttall's cottontails
•creeping voles and long-tailed voles
•yellow-bellied marmots

Bugs
Of all the creeping and flying things that one could mention, there is a creature frequently encountered that is a potential threat to health. This is the western black-legged tick, *Ixododes pacificus.* In regional studies, up to 3% of captured ticks carried the spirochete bacteria which causes Lyme disease. The tick larvae live on rodents and reptiles, and ingest the bacteria from them. The western fence post lizard is a common host of the tick larvae, but may not harbor the disease because the "cold-blooded" reptile environment is not favorable to the spirochete. Ticks wait on low vegetation with hooked legs outstretched, ready to catch a host. On a human, they typically climb up to the neck or hairline, and they can crawl about for a few hours looking for the perfect spot to bite. Removing a tick within 24 hours of its bite may prevent transfer of the disease bacteria. (Tick information from TRIP Guide—Borgias 1992)

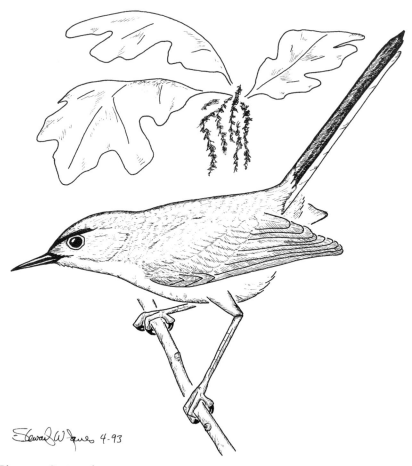

Blue-gray Gnatcatcher

Birds of Table Rock
Dr. Stewart W. Janes

ILLUSTRATIONS BY DR. STEWART JANES

It's quiet as I step out of my car. I can hear the engine pop and crackle as it begins to cool. On the eastern horizon behind Mt. McLoughlin the darkness is fading, and in less than an hour the sun will appear, officially beginning another day on the Table Rocks. However, in the half light, the new day has already arrived for most of the birds, except for the Turkey Vultures who wait for the sun to warm the air and generate the thermals that will enable them to search for the remains the night has left behind. Now is the best time to seek birds in the oak savanna and chaparral that skirt the Table Rocks.

Birding in wooded or shrub-covered habitats can be frustrating. If you want to easily *see* birds, go to the ocean or marsh. On the Table Rocks you must listen. You will hear far more than you see.

On the slopes a Mountain Quail whistles. The loud penetrating call sounds little like the California Quail that also inhabit the area usually lower down nearer people. It took me some time before I finally tracked down the source of this call in a small ravine in eastern Oregon. The tall head plume and rufous sides streaked with white are seldom seen but for a flash as it runs for deeper cover in the chaparral. Though I have heard them many times on the Table Rocks, I have never actually seen one here.

Down the road I hear the soft song of a Western Kingbird. The song of the kingbird is rarely heard after sunrise, and many birders I know have never heard it at all. The faint but pleasant song contrasts with the more familiar call and harsh scold.

Behind me a Western Meadowlark sings loudly atop a ceonothus, proclaiming his rights to all the insects and seeds in this field. I imagine a well-concealed domed nest in a dense patch of grass with a covered path leading away. If this male's territory is rich in food, there may be a another female sitting on a second nest close by. About half of the male meadowlarks have more than one mate. Polygyny (one male and several females) is common among birds, especially those that inhabit early successional stages such as grasslands and marshes. Here the environment is changing quickly as the dying vegetation enriches the soil. The changes the grasses and flowers bring to the soil will ensure their eventual demise as new kinds of plants invade to take advantage of the improved soil. In such a rapidly changing environment (ecologically speaking), some areas abound in food while others are poor. A female meadowlark must decide whether she will be able to raise more young by sharing resources with another female on a rich territory or by living as the sole female on a relatively poor territory. The wisdom of her choice may determine whether or not it will be her offspring that are singing in this field in years to come. The Red-winged Blackbird is another species in the Rogue Valley that is often polygynous.

Despite the scarcity of water, the Table Rocks support a wide range of plant associations, each inhabited by a different assemblage of birds. Each habitat also feels the changing seasons differently and the birds, likewise, respond. I'd like to introduce many of the birds you may hear or see as you might encounter them on a hike up the Table Rocks beginning with the oak savanna and continuing through the chaparral, mixed woodland, the grasslands on the summit and finally the rimrock as you overlook the Rogue Valley below.

Oak Savanna

The oak woodland is a rich habitat and the easiest in which to spot birds. The widely spaced trees and sparse undergrowth of ceonothus and poison oak do not impair visibility severely. Oregon white oaks are preferred by many birds because oaks are susceptible to heart rot. A broken limb allows fungi and bacteria to enter the tree quickly softening the wood for a range of hole nesters to excavate or use once the original owner has left. The rot has little effect upon the oak. The abundance of Plain Titmice, Ash-throated Flycatchers, White-breasted Nuthatches, Western Bluebirds, Violet-green Swallows, Vaux's Swifts, and American Kestrels testifies to the importance of these natural cavities in oaks.

When I first visited the oak savanna of the Table Rocks, I was surprised by the number of hole-nesting birds present and the relative scarcity of birds that construct the typical woven, open cup nests that many birds build including the familiar Robin. It is patterns such as this that ecologists are ever alert. Why should the oak savanna be different? The cause (villain?), I suspect, is the Scrub Jay. Scrub Jays are abundant in the oak savanna. The annual crop of acorns is met with raucous joy by families of jays. You can hear them rejoicing in the bounty as their calls roll across the hillsides as they salt away the harvest in a myriad of cracks and crevices to be later consumed in the lean times of winter and early spring. Studies have documented a remarkable ability in jays to remember where they have stored their food. This ensures high survival and high densities of these beautiful birds.

However, many other birds pay the price because Scrub Jays (and all other jays) enjoy nothing better than a fresh omelet in the cool morning air as the sun greets the rimrock. Jays are persistent and thorough in their search for nests. It amazes me that the Blue-gray Gnatcatcher, Black-headed Grosbeak, and Western Wood Peewee can endure in the presence of these birds. Farther north Oregon white oaks extend their range through the Columbia Gorge and north and south a bit along the eastern foothills of the Cascades, but the jays do not follow. In these areas the Western Tanager is one of the most abundant breeding birds. This species is conspicuously absent here in the oak zone of the Rogue Valley possibly due to the vulnerability of its open nest to jays.

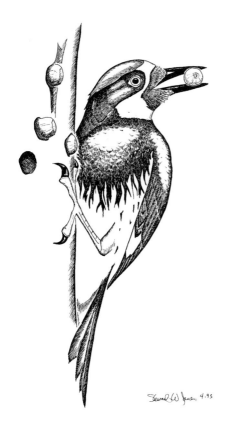

Acorn Woodpecker

Another sound you will likely hear in the oak zone of the Table Rocks is the call of the Acorn Woodpecker. These woodpeckers are unique in many ways. While nearly all woodpeckers feed on insects and other arthropods, the Acorn Woodpecker is a vegetarian feeding on acorns as their name suggests. At first ornithologists suspected they might actually be feeding on the insects, largely weevil grubs, that live inside acorns. However, careful observation revealed that they actually reject acorns that have been invaded by insects.

Acorn Woodpeckers are also unusual for woodpeckers in that they live in groups composed of up to 15 individuals. If you follow their calls, you stand a good chance of observing these birds high on an exposed trunk or limb. As you watch you may see them bob and chase each other from perch to perch as they greet each other, reinforcing their clown-like appearance. The social units are composed of both breeding individuals and other nonbreeding adults that assist in raising the young. Cooperative breeding such as this not common in our area though both recently fledged young of blue-birds and swallows are known to help feed the young of later clutches of their parents. In other parts of the world, such as Australia, cooperative breeding is more common.

Why any individual should forego the opportunity to breed and contribute young to future generations is of intense interest to biologists, especially among normally solitary woodpeckers. Part of the answer appears to lie in their unique diet. Acorns are available for a limited time each year and are sought after by a variety of animals including insects, squirrels, Scrub Jays, Wood Ducks, deer, and at one time the early human inhabitants of the area. If an animal is to live almost exclusively upon acorns, it must find a way to store and protect them to ensure an adequate food supply throughout the year.

A group of Acorn Woodpeckers stores acorns by the thousands in one or more trees called granaries by ornithologists. Granaries consist of small holes drilled by the woodpeckers to receive and hold acorns and are maintained year after year. Scientists have counted as many as 30,000 holes in a single tree. If you locate a granary, you can be assured of finding Acorn Woodpeckers any time you want. Utility poles often serve as granaries, sometimes to the irritation of the people who own and maintain them.

No woodpecker working alone can establish, provision, and protect a granary. It is not possible to drill a sufficient number of holes to hold a yearlong supply of acorns. Further, when a solitary individual leaves to seek acorns, the granary would be left unprotected. Thus granaries are a vital and limited resource that provides the focus of the social group. A group working together can maintain a granary, and, an individual stands a better chance of success by remaining a nonbreeder and waiting for an opening in another social group than by striking out on its own to face almost certain starvation.

The structure of the social group is interesting. It has been shown genetically that, typically, more than one male and female are involved in producing young. Among the breeding members of the group any male may breed with any female. However, each female attempts to be the sole contributor of eggs to the nest. Upon finding a strange egg in the nest, a female is likely to pick the egg up, remove it from the nest, and destroy it. Then it returns to lay an egg of its own. The next female may repeat the process. This appears to continue until they are not sure whose eggs are whose, and then they peacefully settle down to complete the clutch, incubate the eggs, and raise the young.

Granary Tree, Upper Table Rock.

Chaparral

Chaparral is a Spanish word referring to the thick shrubby vegetation that covers the foothills of California and neighboring areas. It is unusual to find Spanish words applied to places or habitats in Oregon, but it is fitting. In many ways the Rogue Valley includes the northern extension of a typically Californian vegetation type. It is difficult for a native Oregonian to admit that anything in Oregon is Californian in nature.

Situated anywhere else but near the coast, the chaparral would revert to desert. Annual precipitation in chaparral habitats falls within the range of most deserts. Only the moderating influence on temperature of marine air permits a different set of plants to persist. These plants are characterized by small, leathery leaves that limit water loss and facilitate the loss of excess heat. Ceonothus and manzanita are two classic chaparral plants. Furthermore, these plants are adapted to fire, which is an integral part of this community. Either they are adapted to reseed and grow rapidly following a fire or they resprout from energy stores held underground sometimes in specialized structures.

Mediterranean climates are scattered throughout the world (Chile, South Africa, southwest Australia, and the Mediterranean) and the associated vegetation is similar in design each place though the species are only distantly related. Birds communities also show parallels in structure in these widely separated locations. Each place supports a similar number of bird species and there are surprising similarities in the appearance and ecological roles of the various species.

Many chaparral birds reach the northern extent of their distribution here in the chaparral or oak/chaparral habitats of the Rogue Valley or nearly so. Birders from around the state come here to complete their lists. These include the Blue-gray Gnatcatcher, Lesser Goldfinch, Plain Titmouse, California Towhee (formerly Brown Towhee), Acorn Woodpecker, and Anna's Hummingbird. The Wrentit, while it continues north along the Oregon coast in shrubby habitats, inhabits chaparral and continues no farther north in the interior of Oregon. As late as the 1960s the largely non-migratory Anna's Hummingbird was seldom found north of the Rogue Valley, but they have recently extended their range north to British Columbia following the the expanding population of "perpetual flowers" called hummingbird feeders.

Titmice are one of the more easily observed birds in the oak/chaparral zone. Listen and be patient. Mated pairs maintain contact with each other through frequent calls most commonly given when actively foraging in the early morning and again in the late afternoon. Being closely related to chickadees, it is not surprising that many of their calls are chickadee-like in nature. They show little fear as they search for insects among the canopy and will approach quite close.

The California Towhees and Blue-Gray Gnatcatchers are more difficult to observe. Listen for the single metallic call note of the towhee and the short buzzy notes of the gnatcatcher. With a little luck and patience you should be able to spot these birds as well during the spring and summer. Unlike the gnatcatcher, the California Towhee is a resident on the Table Rocks, though it becomes quiet and more elusive during the fall and winter.

There are additional birds species characteristic of the chaparral in California but are not normal inhabitants of the Rogue Valley. As I walk through the chaparral of the Table Rocks I listen and watch for these birds hoping to find the rare visitor. These include the Lawrence's Goldfinch, California Thrasher, and Black-chinned Sparrow.

The Black Phoebe is another bird that continues no farther north than the Rogue Valley. However, it is not located in the chaparral, but instead prefers the riparian vegetation bordering the quiet waters of ponds and lazy streams.

Mixed Woodland

While I rejoice in the abundance and diversity of flowers on the Table Rocks in April, I look forward most to the first two weeks of May. It is then the feathered flowers bloom in greatest abundance on the slopes of the Table Rocks. In addition to the birds that will remain to breed, you will find many who only pause here in their northward journey from their wintering areas in the mountains of western Mexico and central America. You will find brightly colored Western Tanagers, Black-headed Grosbeaks, Lazuli Buntings, and a dazzling array of warblers: Wilson's, Yellow, Hermit, Townsend's, Black-throated Gray, MacGillivray's, Yellow-rumped (formerly Audubon's), Nashville, and Orange-crowned swarming among the expanding leaves of the black oaks and other trees of the mixed woodland. Most will be singing at least an occasional song. In addition, you can find an abundance of less colorful species, including vireos (Solitary, Warbling, and Hutton's), Hermit and Swainson's Thrushes, and a variety of small flycatchers dismissed by even some of the better birders as LGBs (little gray/green birds). These are the "dreaded" members of the infuriating genus, *Empidonax*. Even if you shot them as naturalists did in the days of John James Audubon and held the birds in your hands, expert birders could still carry on a long and heated debate as to which species they had. To make matters worse ornithologists keep making more of them. Most recently, the Western Flycatcher has been found to actually be two species, the Pacific Slope and the Cordilleran Flycatchers. The Pacific Slope Flycatcher breeds on the Table Rocks.

These birds are taking advantage of the explosion of prey that occurs each May on the Table Rocks. The moment the oaks begin to awaken, the insects and spiders are there waiting, the herbivores waiting to draw up the sap and consume the leaves and the predators waiting to harvest their percentage of the plant eaters (and other predators). It is a race against time for many. If you are too slow in completing your life cycle, you will end up a meal for a predator feathered or otherwise. Even if you grow fast the odds are not good. If an insect does manage to evade predation, it may succumb to parasitoids. Many people do not realize the importance of insects, in controlling insect populations mostly tiny wasps, that lay their eggs inside the bodies of other insects.

With oaks there is another reason for insects to hurry their development. Oaks and many other trees produce by-products of their normal metabolic activities called secondary compounds. Many are unpalatable or toxic to herbivorous insects. Oaks create tannins, and as the leaves develop tannins gradually accumulate rendering the leaves inedible to most species. As you look across an oak forest in the summer, it may come as a surprise to realize the rustling canopy of green is untouchable to a great many insects.

The wave of migrant birds in May finds the oaks laden with abundant prey. A few weeks earlier and they would find only a few chilled spiders hidden among the lichens; a few weeks later and they would find a greatly diminished food supply, adequate to sustain the birds that breed here but not the multitude of migrants that pass through each spring.

The fall migration in August and September pales in comparison to the spring migration. You can find scattered tanagers and warblers, mostly Black-throated Gray, Yellow and Yellow-rumped, but you have to hunt. If you wish to find forest birds at this time head for Mt. Ashland or other places above 5,000 feet in elevation. At the higher elevations, spring comes late. While the peak in insect availability on the valley floor is May, you will have to wait until July to see any increase in insect abundance, and it peaks in August. Forest birds travel south high in the mountains to take advantage of this food supply. It surprised me the first time I saw Black-headed Grosbeaks and Wilson's Warblers at timberline.

Before we leave the woodlands, I must alert you to the possibility of seeing a Pileated Woodpecker. They are nowhere abundant, but their presence is always felt. You have a better than even chance of hearing their rich and resonant call echo off the rimrock, often in the distance, sometimes close. They have a way of just appearing. You may hear a scratch on a tree trunk, or a peck or two on a limb. You might not consciously hear a thing, but something tells you to turn around and there it is, brilliant red crest and a flash of white in the wing. For such a large bird, they are surprisingly tame. As long as you talk quietly and make no sudden moves, they tend to dismiss humans as irrelevant along with the other earthbound members of the forest community.

For some reason, Pileated Woodpeckers like rectangles. It would seem much easier to drill a round or oval hole when searching for prey as if it mattered, but this woodpecker prefers to drill rectangular holes. Look for their signature in the snags and fallen logs as you walk the trails. If you are exceedingly fortunate, you may meet this woodpecker at your level. They have a fondness for carpenter ants which are abundant in fallen logs.

Grassland

As you attain the summit of the Table Rocks, you quickly leave the forest and chaparral behind. Instead of being immersed in the vegetation, you now tower above it in the grasslands.

Grasslands are not as structurally complex as shrub lands and forests. Consequently, there are fewer ways in which to make a living. For example, there are no trunks or limbs to investigate for insects or extensive leaf litter to search through. Because of this, grasslands the world over support relatively few species of birds. The typical number of birds species that forage primarily for seeds in a given grassland is three. In rich and tall grasslands you may find a fourth. In resource-poor or abused grasslands, you may only find two. The number is amazingly consistent.

Table Rocks are no different. There are three species you are likely to encounter. The most common species is the Lark Sparrow. If you get a clear view, you can see the beautiful face pattern and the spot on its breast. It is one of the earliest migrants to arrive in the spring, usually appearing in late March. It soon fills the fields with its rich song arising from its perch atop the scattered shrubs.

A second species found around the margins of the grasslands is the diminutive Chipping Sparrow. It arrives later in the spring and sings an almost insect-like trill. The third species is the Western Meadowlark. Though a member of the blackbird family and not a sparrow, the meadowlark feeds extensively on seeds as well as arthropods. Sparrows, too, turn to arthropods in the spring as they seek prey rich in protein for their rapidly growing young. Meadowlarks search for prey by using their long beak as a probe to explore thick clumps of grasses.

The soil on top of the Table Rocks is quite thin. Consequently, the vegetation is sparse. Because the grasslands on the summits are less productive than those around the base of the Table Rocks, the meadowlark is much more common at the lower elevations.

The idea that there are limits to the number of species that may occupy an area has been of interest to ecologists for nearly 40 years. Through field studies we hope to define the rules by which species can or cannot coexist. It is accepted that no species can survive long in the presence of another that feeds on the same prey in the same manner, but just how different must two species be before stable coexistence becomes possible?

Prey size is related to the size of the predator. Larger predators usually seek larger prey. The same principle applies to grassland sparrows. Larger sparrows crack and consume larger seeds (and arthropods). This is a simple consequence of physics. A larger beak with larger muscles can exert greater forces to crack larger seeds. Though a larger sparrow could also feed upon smaller seeds, it usually ignores them since they do not provide sufficient food energy to make it worth the sparrow's time. As a loose rule of thumb, if two ecologically similar species differ in weight by a factor of two, they will select food sufficiently different in size to enable coexistence. This pattern has been described among such diverse bird groups as tropical fruit-eating pigeons, kingfishers, hawks (accipiters), and sparrows.

We see the same pattern in the grasslands here. Lark Sparrows averaging 29 grams are roughly double the mass of Chipping Sparrows averaging 12 grams. The Western Meadowlark is heavier than the 60 grams you might expect, weighing in at about 90 grams. Still, an ecologist feels relatively comfortable with these results. You don't see three species all about the same size inhabiting the grasslands.

In the oak woodland and chaparral we see a similar pattern in winter. Juncos descend from the mountains to live along side the resident towhees. Juncos average 20 grams while the Rufous-sided Towhees weigh almost exactly double at 41 grams. The pattern fails, however, when we consider the California Towhee. It weighs 53 grams making it quite similar to the Rufous-sided Towhee. How these two species coexist is something of a mystery and has been the focus of several studies. They appear to forage in different sites within the chaparral. Rufous-sided Towhees forage more in the dense litter under the shrubs and California Towhees forage more between the shrubs. Whether this is difference enough, we don't know. There are always questions left to be answered.

The pattern repeats itself again among the flycatchers of the oak savanna. Ash-throated Flycatchers (27 grams) are double the size of Western Wood Peewees (13 grams).

Raven babies in nest on pinnacle ledge, Upper Table Rock.

Rimrock

The goal for many hikers is to eat lunch sitting on the edge of the rimrock overlooking the valley and river below. I, too, enjoy the feeling of being above the forest and looking down on the canopy. It's not often you can observe a soaring Red-tailed Hawk from above and appreciate the brightly-colored tail highlighted against a green background. The rimrock is the focus of activity for many bird species. In spring and summer loose flocks of Violet-green Swallows wheel both above and beneath you. They nest in the crevices of the rimrock and in cavities in the oaks on the slopes below.

If you look and listen carefully, you will note Vaux's Swifts high above the swallows. They have a shorter arm and longer hand than swallows enabling them to flap faster and attain greater speeds. Whereas the swallows remind me of skiiers slaloming down the slopes, swifts fly a much more direct path. I marvel at their ability to single out flying insects and maneuver to make successful captures at such speeds. Their eyes must also have remarkable abilities to adjust their focus to track rapidly approaching prey. I reflect on my experiences with bugs while riding a bike as well as bugs impacting the windshield of my car and continue to wonder.

Like their eastern counterpart, the Chimney Swift, Vaux's Swifts nest in chimneys. Before chimneys they nested in hollow oaks whose tops have fallen and still do. Their nests are attached to the inside of the trunk near the bottom of the cavity. I have located nests that were beneath ground level at the bottom of a hollow tree. If you attempt to peer into one of their nests, the young begin hissing in the darkness in an unbirdlike manner that apparently serves to discourage potential predators.

If you are visiting the Table Rocks in spring or early summer you may be fortunate to observe a newly discovered resident of this area, the White-throated Swift. White-throated Swifts are larger than Vaux's Swifts, and the bold black and white pattern is reminiscent of a killer whale. These birds are sparse inhabitants of eastern Oregon found in local breeding colonies. They were discovered for the first time in Jackson County in 1991 and probably breed in the rimrock of the Table Rocks. Be careful not to confuse them with the Violet-green Swallows.

One of the most obvious residents of the rimrock are Turkey Vultures. They roost in great numbers on the Table Rocks, and some undoubtedly nest there in cavities in the cliffs or inside hollow logs on the forest floor below. As you approach the rim from the top, approach slowly. Often you can get quite close to several of these birds as they rest along the cliffs. I know of few places better to actually see the bare, red skin of their head and their yellow beak. Even if you fail to find perched birds, sit down and wait. Patience is usually rewarded, and vultures will glide past along the rim at about eye level, often at very close range.

Relatively few birds have heads lacking feathers, and considering the benefits of insulation and keeping one's head warm in cold weather, it's a fair question to ask why it might be beneficial for a bird to ever lack head feathers. Turkeys lack head feathers, and the explanation here apparently lies with a turkey's concept of beauty. A bumpy, wattled head with multi-colored skin is apparently an object of great beauty in the turkey world. The bumpier, more outrageously colored the head, the more mates it attracts. Turkeys have been successfully introduced in the Rogue Valley and should be watched and listened for on the Table Rocks.

A different explanation applies to the vulture. It is a question of health. If a bird's idea of fine cuisine is slightly putrid, sun-warmed road kill, it must deal with the decay organisms that pose a risk of disease. Feathers quickly become matted with fluids and tissues from its meal especially if it is probing deep into the carcass. It is much easier to clean bare skin than fouled feathers. Moreover, cleansing ultraviolet light from the sun which kills many microorganisms cannot penetrate feathers but can work easily on bare skin.

The amount of bare skin of a bird of prey's head can be used to assess the amount of carrion in its diet. Most hawks and falcons have little or no bare skin on their head and rarely consume carrion. Golden Eagles do eat remains of dead organisms especially in winter when prey is less abundant, and they tend to have few feathers between the beak and eye. Bald Eagles feed more extensively on carrion and have more extensive bare patches of skin on their face. Caracaras of the desert southwest and Florida continue in this trend of greater carrion feeding paralleling reduced facial feathers. Finally, we arrive at vultures and condors which feed exclusively on nonliving prey, and their heads are almost devoid of feathers.

Despite their excellent design for soaring, vultures have surprisingly small flight muscles, and they cannot sustain flapping flight for very long.

Instead, much of the flight musculature has been replaced by tendons which do not fatigue. Once the wings are extended, they can hold them in position while expending a minimum amount of energy. Instead of providing the energy for flight through their own efforts, they gain the energy they need by finding areas of rising air and utilizing its energy. Even the characteristic V-shape of the wings helps in energy conservation. If a gust rocks a vulture to one side, the wing on the lower side becomes parallel to the ground increasing lift on the wing. The wing on the upper side loses lift as the angle relative to the ground increases. Thus the lower wing rises, returning the vulture to the original equilibrium position. In the process, the vulture has not had to move a single muscle.

The Table Rocks are perfectly situated for Turkey Vultures. The rimrock provides easy takeoff even in cold and still air. Further, much of the rimrock faces south and east which catches the early morning sun. As the sun strikes the ground, a thin layer of air near the surface heats first, and this air is usually laden with moisture. The moist, heated air is quite buoyant but remains trapped temporarily under the cooler and denser air above it. Any hill or rise allows the buoyant air to rise by creeping up the slope and accumulate at the high point until there is a sufficient mass of air to rise away from the earth and break free. The bubble of air is called a thermal and has its own internal circulation pattern. As the thermal rises slowly, air inside the thermal near the center is rising more quickly. The rising air inside the thermal returns to the bottom near the outside edge. The effect is like a huge doughnut lying flat and rolling up on the inside and down on the outside. Vultures and other birds such as hawks, eagles, and gulls know how to locate thermals and take advantage of them. Once inside a thermal all you have to do is turn a circle small enough to remain within the region of rising air.

By facing south and east, the Table Rocks generate numerous thermals beginning early in the morning and make it attractive to vultures. As a consequence, the Table Rocks have served as a gathering place for vultures both on their northward and southward migration for hundreds and likely thousands of years. I suspect a majority of the vultures breeding west of the Cascades in Oregon, Washington, and British Columbia all pause at the Table Rocks.

When Lewis and Clark visited Oregon in 1804, they encountered California Condors feeding on spawned out salmon along the lower reaches of the Columbia River. It was probably an annual occurrence for many of these birds to travel north from breeding areas in California to take advantage of the abundant source of food. I suspect that condors once found the Table Rocks to be as convenient a stopping over point in their migration as Turkey Vultures do today. I try to imagine what it would be like to sit along the rim eating lunch and have a condor or two sail past at eye level just beyond reach.

Before you leave, listen for an imp of a bird that is occasionally encountered on the Table Rocks but is otherwise rare west of the Cascades, the Rock Wren. The Rock Wren scurries up and down the cliff face investigating each crack and cranny probing crevices with its long and slender bill. If it notices your presence, it may approach you with an accusing call note asking if you have permission to pass.

As you descend the trail expect to experience a different view of the birdlife. If you began your hike early, it will be quieter now. The morning chorus has faded. Even in the winter there is a brief period of calling that soon fades into quieter explorations for food. If you walk silently, this is often the best time to approach foraging birds such as the Ash-throated Flycatcher, Plain Titmouse and Blue-gray Gnatcatcher. They can be absorbed in their activities and ignore you. Before you leave the Table Rocks, pause and listen for one last call of the Mountain Quail or Pileated Woodpecker descending from the hillside.

Cliffside lunch break, BLM/TNC hike, Upper Table Rock.

Checklist

Type of Bird	Surrounding Farmland	Oak Savanna	Chaparral	Mixed Woodland	Grassland
❏ Great Blue Heron	X				
❏ Green-backed Heron	X				
❏ Canada Geese	X				
❏ Mallard	X				
❏ Wood Duck	X				
❏ Turkey Vulture	X	X	X	X	X
❏ Red-tailed Hawk	X	X	X	X	X
❏ Cooper's Hawk		X		X	
❏ Sharp-shinned Hawk		X		X	
❏ Northern Harrier	X				X
❏ Prairie Falcon	X				X
❏ American Kestrel	X	X			X
❏ Ring-necked Pheasant	X				X
❏ California Quail	X	X	X		
❏ Mountain Quail			X	X	
❏ Common Nighthawk	X	X			
❏ Mourning Dove	X	X			X
❏ Band-tailed Pigeon				X	
❏ Great Horned Owl	X	X		X	
❏ Screech Owl	X	X		X	
❏ Pygmy Owl				X	
❏ Barn Owl	X				
❏ Killdeer	X				
❏ Common Snipe	X				
❏ Anna's Hummingbird	X	X	X	X	
❏ Rufous Hummingbird			X	X	
❏ Vaux's Swift	X	X		X	
❏ White-throated Swift	(rimrock only)				
❏ Common Flicker	X	X	X	X	X
❏ Pileated Woodpecker				X	
❏ Red-breasted Sapsucker	X				
❏ Downy Woodpecker	X	X		X	
❏ Hairy Woodpecker				X	
❏ Acorn Woodpecker			X	X	
❏ Lewis' Woodpecker			X	X	
❏ Ash-throated Flycatcher		X	X	X	
❏ Olive-sided Flycatcher				X	
❏ Western Wood Peewee	X	X		X	
❏ Dusky Flycatcher		X	X		
❏ Pacific Slope Flycatcher	(formerly Western)			X	
❏ Western Kingbird	X	X			X
❏ Willow Flycatcher				X	
❏ Tree Swallow	X				
❏ Violet-green Swallow	X	X	X	X	

Permission to duplicate.

Type of Bird	Surrounding Farmland	Oak Savanna	Chaparral	Mixed Woodland	Grassland
❑ Cliff Swallow	X	X	X		
❑ Barn Swallow	X	X	X		X
❑ Steller's Jay				X	
❑ Scrub Jay	X	X	X		
❑ American Crow	X				
❑ Common Raven				X	
❑ Black-capped Chickadee				X	
❑ Plain Titmouse		X			
❑ Bushtit		X	X	X	
❑ Red-breasted Nuthatch				X	
❑ White-breasted Nuthatch		X		X	
❑ Brown Creeper				X	
❑ Rock Wren	*(rimrock only)*				
❑ Bewick's Wren		X	X	X	
❑ House Wren	X	X			
❑ Winter Wren				X	
❑ Golden-crowned Kinglet		X		X	
❑ Ruby-crowned Kinglet	X	X		X	
❑ Blue-gray Gnatcatcher		X	X		
❑ Western Bluebird	X	X			
❑ Swainson's Thrush				X	
❑ Hermit Thrush				X	
❑ American Robin	X	X		X	
❑ Varied Thrush				X	
❑ Wrentit		X	X		
❑ Water Pipit	X				
❑ Cedar Waxwing	X			X	
❑ European Starling	X	X			
❑ Solitary Vireo				X	
❑ Hutton's Vireo				X	
❑ Warbling Vireo		X		X	
❑ Orange-crowned Warbler		X		X	
❑ Nashville Warbler				X	
❑ Yellow Warbler	X	X		X	
❑ Yellow-rumped Warbler	X	X		X	
❑ Black-throated Gray Warbler		X		X	
❑ Townsend's Warbler				X	
❑ Hermit Warbler				X	
❑ MacGillivray's Warbler		X		X	
❑ Wilson's Warbler		X		X	
❑ Western Tanager		X		X	
❑ Black-headed Grosbeak		X		X	
❑ Lazuli Bunting	X	X		X	
❑ Rufous-sided Towhee	X	X	X	X	
❑ California Towhee		X	X		
❑ Chipping Sparrow	X	X			X

Permission to duplicate.

Type of Bird	Surrounding Farmland	Oak Savanna	Chaparral	Mixed Woodland	Grassland
❏ Vesper Sparrow					X
❏ Lark Sparrow	X	X			X
❏ Savannah Sparrow	X				X
❏ Fox Sparrow				X	
❏ Song Sparrow	X			X	
❏ Lincoln's Sparrow	X				
❏ Golden-crowned Sparrow	X	X	X	X	
❏ White-crowned Sparrow	X			X	
❏ Dark-eyed Junco	X	X	X	X	
❏ Red-winged Blackbird	X				
❏ Western Meadowlark	X	X			X
❏ Brewer's Blackbird	X	X			X
❏ Brown-headed Cowbird	X	X	X	X	
❏ Northern Oriole	X	X			
❏ Purple Finch		X		X	
❏ House Finch	X	X			
❏ Pine Siskin		X		X	X
❏ Lesser Goldfinch	X	X	X		X
❏ American Goldfinch	X	X	X		X
❏ Evening Grosbeak				X	
❏ House Sparrow	X				

Permission to duplicate.

Happy patch of Balsamroot (Sunflower Family)—June, Lower Table Rock.

FLORA

ILLUSTRATIONS BY DR. FRANK LANG

As hikers ascend the trail, they will pass in and out of sunny and shady areas. Depending on the soil, slope aspect, and climate, the plants will be different in the sun than those in the shade. These are plant communities: different plants with the same needs bunching together. When the environment changes, so do the types of plants. Another term used is plant associations, but it is a much more complex concept.

Being part of a community requires give and take on the part of the vegetation; dependence on certain plants is needed as is the ability to put up with other plants.

The communities are arranged in layers, subdivisions based on plant height, and trees are usually the dominant species, with shrubs next, then herbs.

Unfortunately, all the communities must be considered seminatural in character due to human activities. (Franklin and Dryness 1988) This is because even the prehistoric Indians here influenced nature by purposely setting fires.

We will first look at the communities as a whole and then scrutinize the individual layers.

The Communities

There are three basic vegetation types* on both Rocks which will be described in order as if ascending the trails:
1. Oak Woodlands
    A. white oak savanna
    B. black oak & madrone mixed woodland
2. Chaparral
3. Mounded Prairie
    A. mound
    B. intermound
    C. vernal pool

Oak Woodlands

The Rogue River Valley is enclosed by the mountain ranges all around it, causing it to be relatively warm and dry. It is called an "Interior Valley," and one of the conspicuous features of this zone is the oak woodland. These oak stands, groves, and savannas have been described as the driest *forested* formation. (Franklin and Dryness 1988)

The **savanna** is the widespread open canopy white oak forest over grassland. (Borgias 1979) It is found at the lower elevations of the trails. Overgrazing and human activity has caused the native perennial bunchgrasses to be invaded and dominated by alien annual grasses. Natural fires are needed to keep the brush down in the savanna.

*These types are a simplified and differing breakdown of those communities recognized by the Oregon Natural Heritage Program. For the in-depth discussion, see *Kalmiopsis*, Journal of the Native Plant Society of Oregon, V3 1993.

The other plants that stick with the white oak on these sunny slopes are buckbrush, deerbrush, manzanita, madrone, mountain mahogany, and poison oak species. The association of white oak and buckbrush tends to grow on the north facing slopes, with the white oak, poison oak, and grass association on the south. Poison oak has replaced buckbrush as the dominant shrub in some places, also as a result of grazing. (It does not taste as good!) Common flowers to the oak savanna are the Henderson fawn lily, brodiaea, buttercups, hound's tongue, red bells, shooting stars, cat's ear, and camas.

About midway up The Rocks and just under the summit on the talus slopes, the **black oak and madrone mixed woodland** is entered. The soil is different here, well-drained and loamy. The canopy created by the sun-loving big madrones and their co-dominant black oaks helps keep this area cooler and more moist than the savanna. Black oak seedlings prefer the woods, while the white oaks prefer the open fields. (Bernstein 1988) Ponderosa pines are also found in this woodland as a subdominant overstory species, but they do not like either crowding or too much shade. The conifers (the ponderosa pine, douglas-fir and incense cedar) may eventually replace the madrones and black oaks as the dominant species if fire does not intervene. (Borgias 1990)

Shrubs found here include Oregon grape, Fremont silk-tassel, elderberry, serviceberry, honeysuckle, and manzanita. Unlike its cousin buckbrush, deerbrush seems to prefer the partial shade. Common flowers include several of the sunflower species, little woodrose, star flower, and false Solomon's seal.

Chaparral

This is the sclerophyllous, or "hard-leaved" shrub community, and these shrubs stand out in the highest temperatures in rocky, shallow, low fertility soil. (See page 67.) This community is located around the perimeter of The Rocks and overlaps its area with the oak woodlands. The two dominant species are buckbrush and manzanita, and certain areas of the trail give the impression of passing through a narrow corridor.

The term chaparral comes from the Spanish chaparro, which means scrub oak. Because the shrubs are so jammed together, the horseback riders had to wear chaparreros or "chaps!"

Fire is needed to keep the chaparral from becoming stagnant, as both buckbrush and manzanita species need a hot fire to germinate their seeds. These shrubs even make it easy for a fire to get going, by emitting volatile oils and creating a readily burned fuel layer. (Latimer 1980) Joyce Bork, who wrote her master's thesis about Upper Table Rock, mentioned that the apparent decline of mountain mahogany and Fremont silk-tassel in the chaparral may be a result of too few fires. The buckbrush will also become too tall, and will stop producing live growth unless regenerated by fire.

The prettiest time in this community is when the shrubs themselves are in bloom, during March and April. The scent of the buckbrush is especially heavy and sweet. The manzanita is full of little pink bells. Look for camas, fawn lilies, brodiaea, desert parsley, and shooting star amongst the chaparral.

Mounded Prairie

The lumpy appearance of the summits of The Rocks is due to a phenomenon called patterned ground or mima mounds. There are several theories to explain the mounds, and three of them especially apply to The Rocks. The first is the "frost heave" theory, which states that Ice Age freezing and thawing has caused the ground to expand and contract so much that the big rocky pieces roll off into depressions (intermound area), leaving the finer soil in a pile. Another theory is that constant gopher activity forms the mounds. You will see lots of evidence of that! It has been determined that thirty gophers can move 3.2 tons of soil per acre per month! (Bork 1978) Mounding evidently only occurs when there is thin soil over dense ground or rock, and the water table rising nearly to the surface leaves the gophers very little headroom.

The third possibility is that the bunchgrasses catch windblown soil and silt, causing an accumulation. Bob Hawkins, who has led hikes for scout and church groups on The Rocks for 15 years, witnessed tiny whirlwinds or "go-devils" pick up dirt and grass and create piles over a five-hour period one spring.

During the winter months, certain depressions in the intermound areas collect water, forming vernal pools.

The mounds, intermound spaces, and vernal pools have distinct environments and, therefore, distinct plant communities.

Mound Community

The mounds have a greater soil depth (30 to 50 inches) than the intermound areas and have a loam to clay-loam soil. Again, the mounds were formerly dominated by native perennial bunchgrasses, but they have been crowded out by introduced annual grasses. Human activities such as off-road vehicle use, horseback riding, construction of roads and an airstrip, grazing and, of course, hiking, have introduced alien plant species, especially the star thistle. A former landowner dropped grass, wildflower seeds, and fertilizer by plane approximately 40 years ago over Lower Table Rock. It has been speculated that some landed on Upper Table Rock and the Agate Desert also. There had been no studies of The Rocks prior to this time to help differentiate which plants were native and which were not, and there has never been a study comparing Upper's vegetation to Lower's.

Of 60 species collected on the summit of Lower Rock, 30% of the species occurs on the mounds.

Grasses dominating the mounds include hairy and soft chess (introduced annuals) and foxtail fescue. Other grasses include shining peppergrass, flat pod, wild oat, and medusa-head grass, another undesirable invading species. Of the flowering plants, on Upper the annuals and perennials occur in equal numbers. On Lower, the ratio of annuals to perennials is 3.5:1. (Kranz and Richter 1980) Because of its depth, mound soil can hold moisture and therefore sustain flowering plants into the summer longer than the other grassland areas. Flowers include miniature lupine, blue-eyed Marys, fiddlenecks, and popcorn flowers.

Intermound Community-Rocky Scabland

The intermound soil is thin, 2–8 inches deep, with lots of exposed rocks, and consists of silts and clays. There are twice as many annuals as perennials in this community, because there is not enough space for the extensive root systems which perennials need to survive drought.

The rocky scabland is fields of rocks amongst a moss covered soil layer that is less than an inch thick. This area is extremely fragile and overturning the rocks exposes plant roots that need their protection. (Latimer 1990) These roots grow at horizontal angles instead of vertical. (Bork 1978)

The intermound depressions are dominated by goldfields with Wallace's selaginella in the rocky areas. "Selaginella dries and withstands desiccation for months only becoming green and expanding when moisture arrives." (Bork 1978) Wild onions, a grazing favorite, snuggle up to the rocks in the scabland. In moister areas, the moss *Rhacomitrium canescens* occurs. Other plants include poverty clover (cows udders), grass widows, strawberry flowers, and monkey flowers.

According to Kranz and Richter, the intermound species account for 52% of all the species in the grassland on Lower Table Rock. Not bad for such poor soil!

Vernal Pools

The intermound areas that have a greater clay content are not able to drain as fast and consequently hold the rainwater in pools. By definition, a vernal pool is a small body of water that dries up at least once a year. Such pools occur from approximately October to June. This is the only water available to the summits, yet each Rock has a semi-perennial spring located in it's "bowl." (Borgias 1992)

Vernal Pool—April, Lower Table Rock.

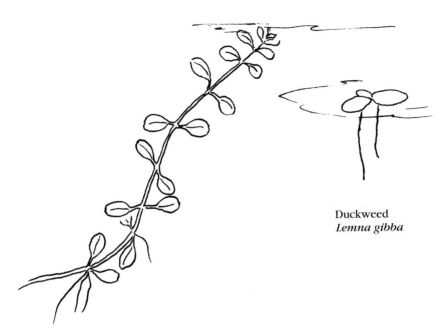

Duckweed
Lemna gibba

Starwort
Callitriche stagnalis

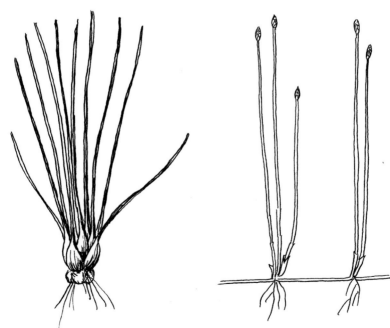

Nuttall's Quillwort
Isoetes nuttallii

Creeping Spike-rush
Eleocharis palustris

VERNAL POOL PLANTS

Mousetail
Myosurus minimus

Woolyheads
Psilocarphus brevissimus

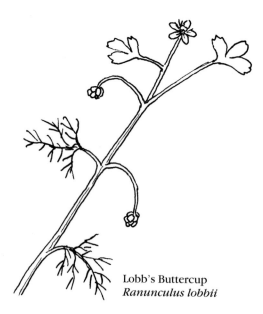

Lobb's Buttercup
Ranunculus lobbii

VERNAL POOL PLANTS

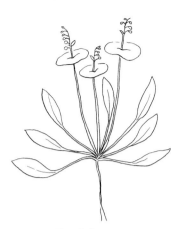

Miner's Lettuce
Montia perfoliata

Lace Pod
Thysanocarpus curvipes

Stork's Bill-Filaree
Erodium circutarium

Shepherd's Purse
Capsella bursa-pastoris

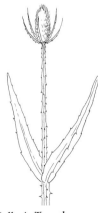

Fuller's Teasel
Dipsacus fullonum

GRASSLAND/WOODLAND PLANTS

Rings of blooming flowers appear as the water evaporates, with annuals dominant. (See page 98.) Early bloomers include the dwarf wooly meadow-foam, mousetail, navarretia, downingia, camas, wooly marbles, and Lobb's buttercup. Lobb's buttercup was on the Oregon Endangered Plant List, and the dwarf wooly meadowfoam is on the federal register, a candidate for the threatened species list, as it is found only on the summit of the two Table Rocks. Creeping spike-rush dominates during the drying process, with fox-tail and hairgrass also blooming in the drying vernal pool. Duckweed and Nuttall's quillwort are the perennials of the vernal pools; this quillwort is considered rare in Oregon.

Plant Community Criteria

Oak woodland-savanna
• Ascending to 3,000 feet
• Average rainfall 15 to 40 inches
• Growing season 6 to 9 months
• 180 to 265 frost-free days
• Mean summer maximum temperature 80 to 90°F, mean winter minimum temperature 29 to 42°F
• Trees 25 to 75 feet tall
• Hot dry summers
• Dense or open woodland with scattered brush and grassland between trees
• Composite community contains both oak parklands of valley floor and pine woodland of surrounding slopes

Grassland
• Low hot valleys of inner Coast Range
• Ascending to approximately 4,000 feet
• Average rainfall 6 to 20 inches
• Growing season 7 to 11 months
• 205 to 325 frost-free days
• Mean maximum summer temperature 88 to 102°F
• Winter rain and hot dry summers
• Open treeless grasslands
• Rich display of flowers in wet springs
• Local habitats with distinctive floras

(Taken with minor variations from *Lower Table Rock Preserve: A Stewardship Master Plan*, Ronald Kranz and John Richter, 1980.)

Ecology

The differing plant communities on The Rocks are not as stable as they seem. There is a process called succession, by which various factors cause the environment and corresponding ecosystems to change and replace one another until a constant state of being is finally reached (a "climax community"). Crumbling rock disintegrates into soil, mixing with plant debris and becoming richer. Disturbances (manmade or natural) also hasten change, for the good or bad. Grazing is a disturbance, as is fire, landslides, logging, etc. There has been a dramatic change in the vegetation of the Willamette Valley since settlement of the 1850's. The pioneers' fire control activities caused the open savannas to become closed forests. "Old *Quercus* (*garryana*-white oak) snags of open-growth form can be found in many foothill *Pseudotsuga menziesii* (Douglas-fir) stands, victims of the conifer seedlings they sheltered." (Franklin and Dryness 1988) In *First Over The Siskiyous*, Jeff LaLande mentions in his notes that the Bear Creek valley once had many open groves of mature ponderosa pine, which the settlers of the 1850's cut down.

While some believe the Rogue Valley chaparral communities are in the climax stage (Franklin and Dryness 1988), others believe the chaparral may need fire for continuance. There is evidence that conifers will eventually dominate the black oak-madrone woodland, and that the talus slopes, given enough deterioration, will support a woodland. (Borgias 1992)

Three men and a cliff. John Bridges, Jeff Gillie, and Jeff Beattie, Upper Table Rock.

Oregon White Oak
Quercus garryana

California Black Oak
Quercus kelloggii

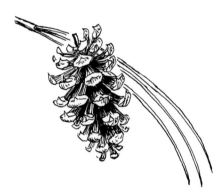

Ponderosa Pine
Pinus ponderosa

Douglas-fir
Pseudotsuga menziesii

Incense Cedar
Calocedrus decurrens

Pacific Madrone
Arbutus menziesii

TREES

TREES

Just six kinds of trees will be encountered along the Table Rocks trails and on their summits. Those shrubs that are big enough to be small trees are listed in the *Shrub* section. The trees are listed in alphabetical order according to their common names.

Douglas-fir *Pseudotsuga menziesii* PINE FAMILY
Douglas-firs are easily identified by flat needles sticking off the twig like a bottlebrush. Older trees have a corky bark with deep furrows. Cones have closed reddish-brown woody scales, and a papery 3-pronged "bract" that projects from between the scales. (It looks like a tongue sticking out.) This tree is second only to the redwoods and sequoias in height, growing fast and reaching as high as 250 feet high. They can live to be 1,000 years old. It is the most adaptable tree, growing in a wide range of environments, and it can survive both drought and fire. It has an intermediate tolerance to shade and tends to become the dominant in oak/madrone woods. This is Oregon's state tree, and it is the most important lumber tree in the nation. (Randall 1981)
Because of its confusing identity, the Douglas-fir name must be hyphenated. It is not a fir, and its botanical name translates to "false hemlock." Classified as a pine, it does not have pine-like cones or needles. (Arno 1977)

California Black Oak *Quercus kelloggii* BEECH FAMILY
The clue to differentiating between this tree and the white oak is the leaves. Black oak leaves have pointed tips! The acorns also provide a clue; they have a deeper cap than do the whites. The black's acorns take two seasons to mature, but they were the Indian's preferred species. The bark tends to be dark brown with deep furrows. They are so slow growing that they may reach 80 feet and live to be 500 years old. This oak tends to prefer "the woods," while the white oaks prefer the open fields. The northernmost range for this primarily California-based species is about Eugene, Oregon.

Incense Cedar *Calocedrus decurrens* CYPRESS FAMILY
This is an evergreen with lacy, scaly needles arranged in flat sprays. It has a purplish-red scaly bark, furrowed when old. Incense cedars can reach 110 feet tall and attain 500 years. The cones are funny little gadgets that resemble a duck's bill when closed and a flying goose when open. (Warren 1981) They have tiny yellow blooms in winter and early spring. While considered a drought resisting tree and less moisture-demanding than other "cedars," this tree hangs out in the shadier areas of the trail. Thick bark at the base makes it fire resistant. This is the cedar from which both pencils and the lining for cedar chests are made. The heartwood is often infected by a fungus, causing a condition known as "pecky cedar," but the wood can be used for paneling and fence posts.

Oregon White Oak *Quercus garryana* BEECH FAMILY
This is the savanna tree: short, thick trunk with a spreading crown. Because it is very shade intolerant, it prefers to stand alone. It produces an inch-long acorn with a shallow cap. Its leaves have rounded lobes, the best feature to distinguish it from the black oak. Its bark is light grayish-brown

with a chalky appearance. It can become 100 feet tall and can live from 350–500 years. It is also called garry oak.

Pacific Madrone *Arbutus menziesii* HEATH FAMILY

This big, beautiful tree is found in the shady areas. Twisted trunks shed red-brown bark, showing the green new bark underneath. Shiny, dark green leaves form an umbrella-like canopy. It is considered a broadleaf evergreen even though it sheds its leaves. It produces an orange-red, mealy, berry-like drupe and white, urn-shaped flowers. Madrones can reach 100 feet tall and live 200 years. Besides being a preferred firewood, there is little commercial use for its lumber, as it splits and warps while curing, and does not have a straight grain.

Ponderosa Pine *Pinus ponderosa* PINE FAMILY

These are tall, open trees with needles 5–10 inches long, green to yellow-green in clusters of three. Its cones have a sharp prickle on the thick end of each scale. The oldest trees have a distinctive bark that looks like jigsaw puzzle pieces. A Ponderosa pine can live to be 400–500 years old. It is able to grow in areas receiving less than 12 inches of rain per year and where the ground surface temperatures reach 160 degrees F! This is due to its ability to put down long roots. One example is an arid grove of four-year-old trees that were only a foot high but had five foot long roots! Their thick bark makes them resistant to death by fire, and they are quick to repopulate a burned over area, receiving the title "pioneer species." Ponderosas need a lot of growing space and are shade intolerant. This major timber species produces a soft wood and the immature (less than 120 years old) wood is the "knotty pine."

Note About the Oaks (Borgias 1979)

The round "balls" that you see on the branches are called oak galls or oak apples. They are caused by a certain kind of wasp that injects its eggs into the branches with its stinger (ovipositor). The oak then develops a tumor, because the wasp DNA mutates the plant cells. The growing larvae use the soft insides for food. If you inspect a downed gall, you may find the tiny hole where the larvae tunneled out.

Buckbrush
Ceanothus cuneatus

White Manzanita
Arctostaphylos viscida

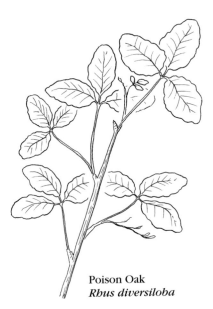

Poison Oak
Rhus diversiloba

SHRUBS

Deerbrush
Ceonothus integerrimus

Fremont Silk-tassel
Garrya fremontii

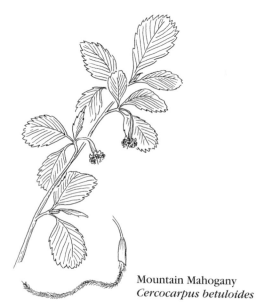

Mountain Mahogany
Cercocarpus betuloides

SHRUBS

SHRUBS

These are arranged alphabetically according to their common names. They may be found on both Rocks unless otherwise stated.

Buckbrush: *Ceanothus cuneatus* BUCKTHORN FAMILY

This bush is the main component of the chaparral and forms those dense thickets that the trail passes through. Grows up to eight feet tall, with grayish leaves and light grayish bark with spiky twigs. It has living foliage all year. It blooms small white to yellow flowers in clusters during March and April. Buckbrush loves dry, gravelly or rocky soils. It is a favorite browse for blacktail deer.

Deerbrush: *Ceanothus integerrimus* BUCKTHORN FAMILY

This Ceanothus species is sometimes called "wild lilac," even though real lilacs are in a different family (Olives). It differs from buckbrush in that it is a more delicate appearing shrub. Deerbrush averages 4–12 feet tall with green to dark green leaves on yellow-green limber branches. The trunk is gray. Its flowers are generally blue but can be pinkish or white and are best described as fluffy or frothy. This shrub blooms later than buckbrush, in May to July. It grows in a variety of soils but seems to prefer the cooler areas of the trail. It also provides an important deer browse.

Fremont Silk-tassel: *Garrya fremontii* SILK-TASSEL FAMILY

This is an erect evergreen shrub which grows up to 10 feet high, with leathery, oval, light greenish-yellow leaves. Has purple-gray flowers on long sprays, blooms from January to April, and has dark blue to blue-black drupes for fruit. Because of its thick, leathery leaves, it is considered a "hard-leaf" or sclerophyllis shrub and is a component of the chaparral. Fremont silk-tassel is also known as bear brush.

Mistletoe: *Phoradendron villosum* MISTLETOE FAMILY

A clue to this plant is its Greek translation: "phor" = a thief, and "dendron" = a tree. This flowering shrub is a parasite that prefers the oaks, sinking its roots under the bark into the cambium layer to steal water. Its sticky seeds are carried to other trees by birds. It produces pinkish white berries. It has silvery green stiff leaves and grows in obvious bundles up in the oak limbs.

Mountain Mahogany: *Cercocarpus betuloides* ROSE FAMILY

This shrub could be placed in the tree category, since it can reach 40 feet in height, and some of the specimens on The Rocks have thick trunks. It is an evergreen, with distinctive serrated dark green leaves. The flowers are described as "funny little shallow creamy bowls at the tops of long narrow tubes," blooming in April to May. (Rowntree 1939) The fruit, which is very noticeable during May to August, resembles delicate pale bean sprouts or feathery tails up to 3 inches long amongst the leaves. The fruit finally float off, carrying the seeds. Its scientific name, in Greek, means shuttle fruit. Hard tack is another name for this shrub. It, too, a good deer browse. Cousins of this plant (Rose family) found on one or both of The Rocks include:

Western Serviceberry: *Amelanchier florida*
Ocean Spray: *Holodiscus discolor*
Klamath Plum: *Prunus subcordata*
Western Chokecherry: *Prunus virginiana*
Little Woodrose: *Rosa gymnocarpa*
Nutka Rose: *Rosa nutkana*
Himalaya Berry: *Rubus thyrsanthus*

Oregon Grape: *Berberis aquifolium* BARBERRY FAMILY

This is an evergreen shrub with dark green, glossy, holly-like leaves. It produces yellow flowers in clusters during March to April and dark blue edible berries. It grows in sun or shade but is considered shade tolerant. Also known as hollyleaf mahonia, it is Oregon's state flower!

Poison Oak: *Rhus diversiloba* CASHEW FAMILY

This is found as an infamous deciduous shrub 3–10 feet high, or as a tree climbing vine. Leaves are in groups of three, lobed, very shiny, reddish-green when new, then all green, turning red and yellow in the fall. Flowers are small, yellowish-green, occurring in clusters around mid April to May. The fruit is a whitish brown smooth dry drupe. Poison oak grows in all types of soils, but likes dry, low to middle elevation (rarely found over 5,000 feet), open areas. The sap of this plant contains an oil, urosiol, which is a severe skin irritant to most people. (The Pomo Indians of Mendocino County, California, are immune to it and use it to cure warts. Whittlesey 1985) The oil is persistent, and unless washed off, contact with it on pets, tools, or clothing will cause a rash long after one has returned from the hike. Breathing smoke from this plant can also be deadly.

White Manzanita: *Arctostaphylos viscida* HEATH FAMILY

This evergreen shrub grows up to 9 feet tall, with whitish-green leathery oval leaves. It has pretty, pinkish urn-shaped flowers in clusters during March and light red pomes that resemble mini apples. Its scientific name means bear grape, because bears love the fruit. White manzanita has dark reddish-brown bark on twisted trunks like its relative, the madrone, although this plant's bark does not peel as much. There are about 50 species of manzanita in North and Central America, most of them on the Pacific coast.

Blue Elderberry: *Sambucus cerulea* HONEYSUCKLE FAMILY

This bush or small tree grows up to 5 feet tall, with small, cream-colored flowers and powdery covered dark blue fruit (which looks light blue en masse). It occurs in the moist woods of Lower Table Rock.

Chaparral Honeysuckle: *Lonicera interrupta* HONEYSUCKLE FAMILY

This shrub is characterized by a woody trunk up to a foot high, with the branches climbing or reclining on bushes, roundish or oblong green leaves, cream to yellow flowers, red berries. It is found in dry thickets.

Pink or Hairy Honeysuckle: *Lonicera hispidula* HONEYSUCKLE FAMILY

A widely branched shrub that can grow 6–20 feet high, this honeysuckle has slender stems, green oblong or oval leaves, pink to purplish red flowers with yellowish insides, and scarlet berries. It is found in thickets and in the oak woodland of Lower Table Rock.

Rabbitbrush: *Chrysothanmus nauseosus* SUNFLOWER FAMILY

This shrub, 1–5 feet high, has yellow flowers and silvery green foliage. The slender, flexible branches are covered with dense, felt-like hairs. Can be found hugging the cliffs of Upper Table Rock. Blooms in August to October.

Grasses

It is not often that I stop and consider that the world as we know it is held together by the grasses. Their network of roots and their tenacity keeps the soil in place and anchors the devices of nature and men. It is also the basic component of the food chain!

The native grasses to the Table Rocks were perennial bunch grasses (bunchgrass). Bunchgrass grows in dense tufts that enlarge year by year. These dominated the mounds on the summits. Since bunchgrass was the preferred food for grazing animals, the mounds became overgrazed and trampled. This set up an imbalance for the not-as-tasty, alien annual grasses to get a foothold. Annuals flower in the spring, set seed for the next year and then die. (Borgias 1979) These invaders came in on the wind, by birds, on hooves and on shoes. Some of the aliens are valuable range plants and may have been introduced on purpose, but others are aggressive and dangerous weeds.

Perennials are alive and green year-round with a life span of over two years. Perennial grasses produce shoots that live over the winter. If the shoot grows up inside the sheaths of the parent stems, a bunchgrass, such as fescue, is formed. If the shoots run along the surface of the soil, a mat is formed, as with Bermuda grass. If shoots run underground, a tough sod is formed, as with the wheatgrasses and Kentucky bluegrass. (Sampson, Chase, and Hedrick 1951)

Low-growing grasses and those with "runners" are more resistant to grazing pressure than are the erect-growing types. (Stechman 1986)

There have been plans to compare the grasslands of Lower Table Rock, which is not being grazed anymore, with Upper Table Rock.

The tables below describe the grasses found on both Rocks, the comments in parenthesis give their value as forage or range plants. The terms are mixed from different systems of rating the grasses, but it is hoped that an idea of their relative usefulness can be formed. A plant considered "dessert" or "ice cream" is one which is found sparingly in the grassland and is prized by livestock above all others! (Sampson, Chase, and Hedrick 1951)

Native Bunchgrasses
Perennials:

California Oatgrass	(dessert)	*Danthonia californica*
Lemmon's needlegrass	(choice)	*Stipa lemmonii*
Idaho fescue	(choice)	*Festuca idahoensis*
rough/pine bluegrass		*Poa scabrella*
Sandberg bluegrass	(good)	*Poa sandbergii*
*Junegrass	(good)	*Koeleria cristata*

*Still found in Agate Desert, may have been present at one time on The Rocks.

Annuals:

Foxtail fescue	(fair)	*Festuca megalura*
Annual Hairgrass	(filler)	*Deschampsia danthonioides*

European or Mediterranean Transplants

Annuals:

Silver Hairgrass	(weed)	*Aira caryophyllea*
Foxtail	(good)	*Alopecurus saccatus*
Wild Oat	(valuable)	*Avena fatua*
Hairy Chess	(weed)	*Bromus commutatus*
Soft Chess	(good)	*Bromus mollis*
Ripgut	(dangerous)	*Bromus rigidus*
Cheatgrass/Downy Chess	(poor)	*Bromus tectorum*
Barnyardgrass	(poor)	*Echinochloa crusgalli*
MedusaHead	(problem weed)	*Elymus caput-medusae*

Winter

Late Spring

THE FOUR SEASONS OF UPPER TABLE ROCK

Summer

Autumn

Rabbitbrush clings to cliff, Upper Table Rock.

TABLE ROCK FLOWER GUIDE
by Shane Latimer

ABRIDGED FROM THE ORIGINAL DOCUMENT

How To Use This Guide

This was produced as a simple guide to the most common wildflowers seen from the trails of both Table Rocks.

While several of the plants may be listed as edible, they may cause severe allergic reactions if simply tasted. Some may require preparation to remove toxins or tastes. Some may have similar looking but deadly relatives! Remember also, these plants are in a preserve and are protected.

To identify a flower, answer these 3 questions:

(1) *What color is it?*
- Determine the dominant color and turn to the appropriate COLOR section.
- For flowers with more than one color, pick the color that makes up most of the flower, especially the petals. It will probably be listed under both colors.

(2) *What kind of habitat or plant community is it in?*
- After finding the proper COLOR section, decide what kind of habitat the flower is in. A description of habitats is found at the beginning of the *Flora* Section. Habitats and communities:
  - Savanna/Grassland
  - Woodland
  - Chaparral
  - Rock/Scabland
  - Pool/Wet Areas
- Flowers often occur in a number of areas, so don't worry about "gray areas" too much. For example, a flower found between woodland and grassland habitats should be listed under both.

(3) *What is different or special about the flower?*
- Under each flower name, below the habitat type, there is information that should help identify the flower. *The number of petals a flower has is especially important.* Blooming time may also be a helpful guide.
- Use a process of elimination.

WHITE FLOWERS

A—Death Camas *Zygadenus venenosus*; B—Dwarf Wooly Meadowfoam *Limnanthes floccossa ssp. pumila*; C—False Solomon's Seal *Smilacina racemosa*; D—Prairie Star *Lithophragma sp.*; E—Strawberry Flower *Hesperochiron pumilus*; F—Yarrow *Achillea millefolium*; G—Henderson's Stars *Trileleia hendersonii*; H—Popcorn Flower *Plagiobothyrus sp.*

❦ ❦ ❦ WHITE FLOWERS ❦ ❦ ❦

Savanna/Grassland

Blue-eyed Marys/Chinese Pagodas *Collinsia sp.* SNAPDRAGON FAMILY
5 petals united to form 2 lips, an upper and a lower. The heads of flowers are in tiered clusters, the upper petals being white and the lower blue. Blooms in March and April.

Death Camas *Zygadenus venenosus* LILY FAMILY
Tiny, cream-colored flowers clustered at end of a stem about a 1/2–1 1/2 feet tall. Considerably smaller than the common camas, but bulbs are so similar as to be easily confused, with possibly deadly results. Blooms late April through May.

Draba *Draba verna* MUSTARD FAMILY
4 tiny petals arranged in the shape of a maltese cross. A very common tiny flower, often in dense carpets. Blooms in March and April.

Henderson's Stars *Trileleia hendersonii* LILY FAMILY
6 petals, joined at the base, white to pale yellow, with a green to purple mid-vein on each petal. Clusters of flowers at the top of foot high stems. Limited growing area from Northern California up to Lane County. Formerly Henderson's brodiaea. Blooms March to August.

Hyacinth Brodiaea *Brodiaea hyacinthina* LILY FAMILY
6 petals. Has a long stalk topped with a cluster of flowers with large petals. Blooms in March.

Lace Pod *Thysanocarpus curvipes* MUSTARD FAMILY
4 petals arranged in the shape of a maltese cross. The seed pod has a lace pattern at its edges. The plant is somewhat hairy. Blooms in April.

Lepidium/Shining Peppergrass *Lepidium nitidum* MUSTARD FAMILY
4 petals arranged in the shape of a maltese cross. The oval seedpods are smooth and shiny. Blooms in March and April.

Lupine *Lupinus sp.* PEA FAMILY
Pea-like flowers, mostly blue with white. Usually found on mounds, this plant is very common. Distinctive fan-like leaves and pea-pod fruit. Blooms in April and May.

Popcorn Flower *Plagiobothyrus* and *Cryptanthea sp.* BORAGE FAMILY
5 petals, often fused toward the center. Small but very common flower often has a ring of yellow around its center. Blooms in April and May.

Prairie Stars *Lithophragma sp.* SAXIFRAGE FAMILY
5 petals, forming the shape of a star. The "stars" are formed at the top of the flowering stalk. Blooms in March.

Saxifrage *Saxifraga sp.* SAXIFRAGE FAMILY
5 petals. The flowers are arranged in a loose cluster on a naked 1-foot stem above a rosette of broad leaves at the soil surface. Blooms in March and April.

❦ WHITE FLOWERS (Cont'd.)

Shepherd's Purse *Capsella bursa-pastoris* MUSTARD FAMILY
4 petals arranged in the shape of a maltese cross. The seedpod is heart-shaped and looks like a shepherd's purse. The flower is not very showy. Blooms in early April.

Strawberry Flower *Hesperochiron pumilus* WATERLEAF FAMILY
5 united petals. A low-lying plant with a nickel-sized flower, the flower white with a yellow center, often with streaks of red or purple, fading to pink. Blooms in April.

Yampa *Perideridia gairdneri* CELERY FAMILY
5 very tiny petals. The leaves of this plant are very narrow. The flowers are born on small stalks of equal length that all attach at the same point (an umbel, think of umbrella) to another, larger stalk.

Yarrow *Achillea millefolium* SUNFLOWER FAMILY
This plant looks like a small fern (very finely divided leaf) and smells of menthol when crushed. It also has tall flower stalks with multiple heads. Blooms in May and June.

Woodland

Bedstraw *Galium aparine* COFFEE FAMILY
4 petals, united toward the center. Bedstraw has whorled leaves and 4-edged, square stems. It is very clingy, caused by tiny hook-shaped hairs. Blooms in May.

Cat's or Kitten's Ears *Calochortus tolmiei* LILY FAMILY
3 petals. Has a large flower that is fuzzy on the inside. Its bulb was used by the Takelma as a food. May be tinted rose to purple. Blooms in late April and May.

False Solomon's Seal *Smilacina racemosa* LILY FAMILY
6 tiny petal-like segments. They form a dense cluster of tiny spiky blossoms at the end of a long, single, unbranched stem of alternate, shiny green leaves. Produces edible red berries, favorite of bears. Blooms in April.

Starflower *Trientalis latifolia* PRIMROSE FAMILY
6 petals, pointed and symmetrical, like a star. Low growing, small plant, leaves occur in a whorl below the flower. May be tinged pink in center. Blooms in April.

Chaparral

Chickweed *Cerastium nutans* PINK or CARNATION FAMILY
5 petals with deep notches, often making the flower look like it has ten petals. Not a very obvious plant, less than 6 inches tall. Blooms in early April.

☙ WHITE FLOWERS (Cont'd.)

Pool/Wet Areas

Dwarf Wooly Meadowfoam
Limnanthes floccossa ssp. pumila MEADOWFOAM FAMILY
5 petals. A low-lying plant with hairy, dime sized flowers. A rare species found only on the tops of the two Table Rocks; an endemic species. Blooms in April.

Navarretia *Navarretia sp.* PHLOX FAMILY
5 petals forming a trumpet-shaped flower. The flowers arise from a stickery and wooly head. Blooms in late April and May.

Popcorn Flower *Plagiobothyrus* and *Cryptanthea sp.* BORAGE FAMILY
5 petals, often fused toward the center. Small but very common flower often has a ring of yellow around its center. Blooms in April and May.

Sandwort *Arenaria californica* PINK or CARNATION FAMILY
5 petals. Small plant with delicate, wiry stems, often mixed with the goldfields. Blooms in April.

Saxifrage *Saxifraga sp.* SAXIFRAGE FAMILY
5 petals. The flowers are arranged in a loose cluster on a naked 1-foot stem above a rosette of broad leaves at the soil surface. Blooms in March and April.

Woolyheads or Wooly Marbles
Psilocarphus brevissimus SUNFLOWER FAMILY
5 petals. A low, inconspicuous plant with wooly leaves and flower heads (wool hides the flower) and forms dense patches in pool bottoms. Blooms in May.

YELLOW FLOWERS

I—Balsamroot *Balsamorhiza deltoidea*; J—Desert Parsley/Biscuitroot *Lomatium utriculatum*; K—Western Buttercup *Ranunculus occidentalis*/Southern Oregon Buttercup *Ranunculus austro-oraganum*; L—Goldfields *Lasthenia californica*; M—Monkey Flower *Mimulus guttatus*; N—Oregon Sunshine *Eriophyllum lanatum*; O—Senecio/Butterweed *Senecio integerrimus*; P—Tarweed *Madia madioides*.

❦ ❦ ❦ YELLOW FLOWERS ❦ ❦ ❦

Savanna/Grassland

Balsamroot *Balsamorhiza deltoidea* SUNFLOWER FAMILY
8+ petal-like rays. One large flower head at the top of a 1-2 1/2 foot stem. Has arrowhead shaped leaves at its base. Blooms April through July.

Blowwives *Achrachaena mollis* SUNFLOWER FAMILY
The flower-like parts of this plant have 5 papery fins and are clustered at the top of a single leaved stalk. 6-8 inches tall. Blooms in March and April.

Douglas' Violet *Viola douglasii* VIOLET FAMILY
5 petals—2 pointing up, 2 to the side, and one larger lower lip with dark markings near the throat. A low plant with dissected leaves. Blooms in early April.

Foothill Parsley/Desert Parsley/Biscuitroot
Lomatium utriculatum CELERY FAMILY
5 tiny petals. Many tiny flowers are clustered in groups, which are themselves clustered at the tip of a bloom stalk in flattened "umbels" (think umbrella). Blooms in April.

Mule's Ears *Wyethia angustifolia* SUNFLOWER FAMILY
8+ petal-like rays. Large leaves are relatively linear and the plant is not sticky. Distinguished from balsamroot by having leaves on the stem, not all at the base. Blooms May through June.

Oregon Sunshine/Wooly Sunflower
Eriophyllum lanatum SUNFLOWER FAMILY
8-13 petal-like rays, flowers on long, leafless neck. Stems are well-branched clumps, 1/2-3 feet high. Has gray wooly hair on leaves and stem. Blooms in May.

Senecio/Tower Butterweed *Senecio integerrimus* SUNFLOWER FAMILY
5-10 petal-like rays. Flower heads clustered at top of a single "tower-like" stem, 1-3 feet tall. Spoon-like leaves at the base with a few, small, lance-like leaves on the stem. Blooms in May through August.

Spring Gold *Crocidium multicaule* SUNFLOWER FAMILY
8+ petal-like rays. A small single flower (1-4 inches tall) with small, narrow, alternating leaves on the stem and a rosette of larger leaves at the base. Common on the trail and on the tops of the Rocks. Blooms in March and April.

St. John's Wort *Hypericum perforatum* ST. JOHN'S WORT FAMILY
5 petals. A tall plant (2-3 feet) with many flowers. Opposite leaves with tiny clear areas that make the leaf look perforated. An introduced species. Blooms in June. (St. John's Day is June 24)

Star Thistle *Centauria solstitialis* SUNFLOWER FAMILY
This introduced species had spiny flower heads. Has light gray foliage. Blooms from June to October.

❧ YELLOW FLOWERS (Cont'd.)

Tarweed/Madia *Madia madioides* SUNFLOWER FAMILY
8+ petals with maroon centers. The flower has an urn-shaped base. May be 1-2 feet tall and covered in sticky resinous hairs. The Takelmas collected the seeds for flour. Blooms May through June.

Western Buttercup *Ranunculus occidentalis*
Southern Oregon Buttercup *Ranunculus austro-oraganus* BUTTERCUP FAMILY
5 petals and many stamens. These plants have hairy leaves that are divided into three portions. The southern Oregon buttercup, an endemic species, can be identified by the rust color on the underside of the petals. Blooms in April.

Woodland

Balsamroot *Balsamorhiza deltoidea* SUNFLOWER FAMILY
8+ petal-like rays. One large flower head at the top of a 1-2 1/2 foot stem. Has arrowhead shaped leaves at its base. Blooms April through July.

Douglas' Violet *Viola douglasii* VIOLET FAMILY
5 petals—2 pointing up, 2 to the side, and one larger lower lip with dark markings near the throat. A low plant with dissected leaves. Blooms in early April.

Shelton's Violet *Viola sheltonii* VIOLET FAMILY
5 petals—2 pointing up, 2 to the side, and one larger lower lip with dark markings near the throat. It can be discerned from Douglas' violet by having three distinct leaflets, which are themselves divided. Blooms in April.

Spring Gold *Crocidium multicaule* SUNFLOWER FAMILY
8+ petal-like rays. A small single flower (1-4 inches tall) with small, narrow, alternating leaves on the stem and a rosette of larger leaves at the base. Common on the trail and on the tops of the Rocks. Blooms in March and April.

Western Buttercup *Ranunculus occidentalis*
Southern Oregon Buttercup *Ranunculus austro-oraganus* BUTTERCUP FAMILY
5 petals and many stamens. These plants have hairy leaves that are divided into three portions. The southern Oregon buttercup, an endemic species, can be identified by the rust color on the underside of the petals. Blooms in April.

Chaparral

Balsamroot *Balsamorhiza deltoidea* SUNFLOWER FAMILY
8+ petal-like rays. One large flower head at the top of a 1-2 1/2 foot stem. Has arrowhead shaped leaves at its base. Blooms April through July.

Foothill Parsley/Desert Parsley/Biscuitroot
Lomatium utriculatum CELERY FAMILY
5 tiny petals. Many tiny flowers are clustered in groups, which are themselves clustered at the tip of a bloom stalk in flattened "umbels" (think umbrella). Blooms in April.

❦ YELLOW FLOWERS (Cont'd.)

Oregon Sunshine/Wooly Sunflower
Eriophyllum lanatum SUNFLOWER FAMILY
8-13 petal-like rays, flowers on long, leafless neck. Stems are well-branched clumps, 1/2-3 feet high. Has gray wooly hair on leaves and stem. Blooms in May.

Rock/Scabland

Goldfields *Lasthenia californica* SUNFLOWER FAMILY
7+ petals. A small single flower with opposite leaves, occurring in and around the pools on the summits, and in the scablands. Blooms in April.

Monkey Flower *Mimulus guttatus* or *alsinoides* SNAPDRAGON FAMILY
5 petals, the lower forming a large lip with a red dot or dots. This flower is very small, and can often be found in the soil-filled cracks of rocks. Blooms in April.

Spring Gold *Crocidium multicaule* SUNFLOWER FAMILY
8+ petal-like rays. A small single flower (1-4 inches tall) with small, narrow, alternating leaves on the stem and a rosette of larger leaves at the base. Common on the trail and on the tops of the Rocks. Blooms in March and April.

Pool/Wet Areas

Goldfields *Lasthenia californica* SUNFLOWER FAMILY
7+ petals. A small single flower with opposite leaves, occurring in and around the pools on the summits, and in the scablands. Blooms in April.

Monkey Flower *Mimulus guttatus* or *alsinoides* SNAPDRAGON FAMILY
5 petals, the lower forming a large lip with a red dot or dots. This flower is very small, and can often be found in the soil-filled cracks of rocks. Blooms in April.

Spring Gold *Crocidium multicaule* SUNFLOWER FAMILY
8+ petal-like rays. A small single flower (1-4 inches tall) with small, narrow, alternating leaves on the stem and a rosette of larger leaves at the base. Common on the trail and on the tops of the Rocks. Blooms in March and April.

ORANGE AND RED FLOWERS

Q—Columbine *Aquilegia formosa*; R—Fiddleneck *Amsinckia intermedia*;
S—Grand Collomia *Collomia grandiflora*; T—Indian Paintbrush *Castilleja pruinosa*;
U—Red Bells *Fritillaria recurva*; V—Sierra Wallflower *Erysimum perenne*;
W—Mission Bell *Fritillaria lanceolata*.

❧ ❧ ❧ ORANGE FLOWERS ❧ ❧ ❧

Savanna/Grassland

Blowwives *Achrachaena mollis* SUNFLOWER FAMILY
The flower-like parts of this plant have 5 papery fins and are clustered at the top of a single leaved stalk. 6–8 inches tall. Blooms in March and April.

California Poppy *Eschscholzia californica* POPPY FAMILY
4 papery petals. Brilliant yellow-orange flower. Parsley-like leaves. The California state flower. Blooms in late April.

Fiddleneck *Amsinckia intermedia* BORAGE FAMILY
5 petals. Has small orange flowers that unroll like the end of a violin neck. Very hairy. Blooms in April.

Grand Collomia *Collomia grandiflora* PHLOX FAMILY
5 petals and trumpet-like flowers clustered at top of 1–2 1/2 foot stem. Lance-like leaves. Salmon colored petals are an unusual color for a flower! Blooms April through August.

Indian Paint Brush *Castilleja pruinosa* SNAPDRAGON FAMILY
A low but colorful flower. The plant is rounded at the top and the flowers are hidden beneath a three-colored leaf bract which is red, yellow, and green, tip to base respectively. Blooms in late April or May.

Sierra Wallflower *Erysimum perenne* MUSTARD FAMILY
4 papery petals. Flowers clustered at top of a 1/2–2 foot stem. Very showy plant, found in shade under trees. Blooms in May and June.

Woodland

Blowwives *Achrachaena mollis* SUNFLOWER FAMILY
The flower-like parts of this plant have 5 papery fins and are clustered at the top of a single leaved stalk. 6–8 inches tall. Blooms in March and April.

Columbine *Aquilegia formosa* BUTTERCUP FAMILY
5 spurred petals. Nodding flower on end of 1 1/2–3 foot tall stem. Stems arise from dense clumps of basal leaves divided into threes. Blooms in April.

Fiddleneck *Amsinckia intermedia* BORAGE FAMILY
5 petals. Has small orange flowers that unroll like the end of a violin neck. Very hairy. Blooms in April.

Indian Paint Brush *Castilleja pruinosa* SNAPDRAGON FAMILY
A low but colorful flower. The plant is rounded at the top and the flowers are hidden beneath a three-colored leaf bract which is red, yellow, and green, tip to base respectively. Blooms in late April or May.

Sierra Wallflower *Erysimum perenne* MUSTARD FAMILY
4 papery petals. Flowers clustered at top of a 1/2–2 foot stem. Very showy plant, found in shade under trees. Blooms in May and June.

❦ ❦ ❦ RED FLOWERS ❦ ❦ ❦

Savanna/Grassland

Indian Paint Brush *Castilleja pruinosa* SNAPDRAGON FAMILY
A low but colorful flower. The plant is rounded at the top and the flowers are hidden beneath a three-colored leaf bract which is red, yellow, and green, tip to base respectively. Blooms in late April or May.

Owl's Clover *Orthocarpus bracteosus* SNAPDRAGON FAMILY
5 petals united to form 2 lips, an upper and a lower. Flowers in clustered heads, some with purple spots. Very similar to Indian paintbrush. Blooms in late April.

Woodland

Indian Paint Brush *Castilleja pruinosa* SNAPDRAGON FAMILY
A low but colorful flower. The plant is rounded at the top and the flowers are hidden beneath a three-colored leaf bract which is red, yellow, and green, tip to base respectively. Blooms in late April or May.

Red Bells *Fritillaria recurva* LILY FAMILY
6 petals. Plant has 2+ large, impressive, nodding flowers. The petals have yellow spots on the outside and a yellow throat. The Latin "fritillus" (dice box) refers to the checkered petals. "Recurva" refers to the petal edges turning back on themselves. The leaves are lanceolate (long and narrow, lance-like). Blooms in April.

❦ ❦ ❦ GREEN FLOWERS ❦ ❦ ❦

Woodland

Mission Bell *Fritillaria lanceolata* LILY FAMILY
6 petal-like segments and nodding flower. Brownish-purple mottled with greenish-yellow spots. Narrow leaves on upper part of a 1–4 foot stem. Blooms in February.

Pool/Wet Areas

Duckweed *Lemna gibba* DUCKWEED FAMILY
A tiny plant, common in pools, that floats on the surface of the water. It has two leaves, oppositely arranged. Rarely blooms.

Rush *Juncus sp.* RUSH FAMILY
"Rushes are round…" Flowers somewhat unimpressive with six tiny "petals." It looks like a grass but has pointy tips and is not hollow.

❦ ❦ ❦ NO FLOWERS ❦ ❦ ❦

Woodland

Gold Back Fern *Pityrogramma triangularis* TENDER FERN FAMILY
A small fern found in the cracks of rocks. It has triangular fronds that are green on top and gold on the underside.

Rock Fern *Cheilanthes gracillima* TENDER FERN FAMILY
A small, hairy-looking fern that most often grows in the cracks of large rocks.

Licorice Fern *Polypodium glycyrrhiza* RABBIT'S FOOT FERN FAMILY
A small fern (2–4 inch fronds) commonly growing out of the deep moss on rocks.

Rock/Scabland

Gold Back Fern *Pityrogramma triangularis* TENDER FERN FAMILY
A small fern found in the cracks of rocks. It has triangular fronds that are green on top and gold on the underside.

Rock Fern *Cheilanthes gracillima* TENDER FERN FAMILY
A small, hairy-looking fern that most often grows in the cracks of large rocks.

Licorice Fern *Polypodium glycyrrhiza* RABBIT'S FOOT FERN FAMILY
A small fern (2–4 inch fronds) commonly growing out of the deep moss on rocks.

Selaginella/Crucifixion Plant *Selaginella wallacei* SELAGINELLA FAMILY
This moss-like plant grows mainly on and at the edges of rocks. If one looks carefully, one can see the square cones at its tips.

PINK FLOWERS

X—Farewell-To-Spring *Clarkia gracilia*; Y—Grass Widows *Sisyrinchium douglasii*; Z—Henderson's Fawn Lily/Lamb Tongue *Erythronium hendersonii*; AA—Poverty Clover/Cow's Udder *Trifolium depauperatum*; BB—Shooting Star *Dodecatheon hendersonii*; CC—Wild/Dwarf Onion *Allium parvum*; DD—Wild Onion *Allium amplectens*.

❧ ❧ ❧ PINK FLOWERS ❧ ❧ ❧

Savanna/Grassland

Cat's or Kitten's Ears Calochortus tolmiei LILY FAMILY
3 petals. Has a large flower that is fuzzy on the inside. Its bulb was used by the Takelma as a food. May be tinted rose to purple. Blooms in late April and May.

Clarkia/Farewell-to-Spring Clarkia gracilia EVENING PRIMROSE FAMILY
4 showy petals and alternate leaves. Petals often fade, leaving a dark pink band up the center. It is common on the mounds. Blooms in May.

Clover Trifolium sp. PEA FAMILY
Low plant with trifoliate leaves. Small flowers occurring in heads. Blooms in May.

Grass Widows Sisyrinchium douglasii IRIS FAMILY
6 petals forming this star-shaped flower. It has grass or rush-like, single, pointed leaves. Stands clustered in bunches. Blooms in March.

Owl's Clover Orthocarpus bracteosus SNAPDRAGON FAMILY
5 petals united to form 2 lips, an upper and a lower. Flowers in clustered heads, some with purple spots. Very similar to Indian paintbrush. Blooms in late April.

Poverty Clover/Cow's Udder Trifolium depauperatum PEA FAMILY
Small, low-lying plants with tiny, puffed, purple to magenta flowers shaped like upturned cow's udders. Common on tops of The Rocks in depressions. Blooms in April.

Red-Stemmed Storksbill/Filaree Erodium cicutarium GERANIUM FAMILY
5 petals, with finely divided leaves. The flower is dime-sized and the plant is low-growing. The seeds, when on the plant, are long and sharply pointed (the storksbill). Blooms in April.

Rosy Plectritis Plectritis congesta VALERIAN FAMILY
5 petals united into a tube, the multiple flowers united in a dense cluster. Leaves in an opposite arrangement. Common on the tops of the rocks, often forming a ring around wet depressions. Blooms in April.

Shooting Star Dodecatheon hendersonii PRIMROSE FAMILY
5 petals. Has a whorl of basal leaves. The nodding flowers are atop a leafless stalk. The petals are flared back from a black center. Blooms in April.

Woodland

Cat's or Kitten's Ears Calochortus tolmiei LILY FAMILY
3 petals. Has a large flower that is fuzzy on the inside. Its bulb was used by the Takelma as a food. May be tinted rose to purple. Blooms in late April and May.

Clover Trifolium sp. PEA FAMILY
Low plant with trifoliate leaves. Small flowers occurring in heads. Blooms in May.

☙ PINK FLOWERS (Cont'd.)

Henderson's Fawn Lily/ Lamb's Tongue
Erythronium hendersonii LILY FAMILY
6 petals with two opposite, large, blotchy leaves at the base. The flowers are large and nodding (hanging down). A southern Oregon endemic. Blooms in early to mid April.

Poverty Clover/Cow's Udder *Trifolium depauperatum* PEA FAMILY
Small, low-lying plants with tiny, puffed, purple to magenta flowers shaped like upturned cow's udders. Common on tops of The Rocks in depressions. Blooms in April.

Red-Stemmed Storksbill/Filaree *Erodium cicutarium* GERANIUM FAMILY
5 petals, with finely divided leaves. The flower is dime-sized and the plant is low-growing. The seeds, when on the plant, are long and sharply pointed (the storksbill). Blooms in April.

Shooting Star *Dodecatheon hendersonii* PRIMROSE FAMILY
5 petals. Has a whorl of basal leaves. The nodding flowers are atop a leafless stalk. The petals are flared back from a black center. Blooms in April.

Chaparral

Shooting Star *Dodecatheon hendersonii* PRIMROSE FAMILY
5 petals. Has a whorl of basal leaves. The nodding flowers are atop a leafless stalk. The petals are flared back from a black center. Blooms in April.

Rock/Scabland

Grass Widows *Sisyrinchium douglasii* IRIS FAMILY
6 petals forming this star-shaped flower. It has grass or rush-like, single, pointed leaves. Stands clustered in bunches. Blooms in March.

Poverty Clover/Cow's Udder *Trifolium depauperatum* PEA FAMILY
Small, low-lying plants with tiny, puffed, purple to magenta flowers shaped like upturned cow's udders. Common on tops of The Rocks in depressions. Blooms in April.

Wild Onion *Allium parvum* LILY FAMILY
6 petals. Has a short bare stalk (1–3 inches) topped with a cluster of flowers. Early it has onion-like leaves, but always has an onion scent. Blooms in April.

Pool/Wet Areas

Wild Onion *Allium amplectens* LILY FAMILY
6 petals. Has a short bare stalk (1–3 inches) topped with a cluster of flowers. Early it has onion-like leaves, but always has an onion scent. Blooms in April.

❦ ❦ ❦ BLUE/PURPLE FLOWERS ❦ ❦ ❦

Savanna/Grassland

Baby Blue Eyes *Nemophila pedunculata* WATERLEAF FAMILY
5 petals and opposite leaves. Low and slightly succulent, its usually found on gopher mounds. Blooms in April.

Blue-Eyed Grass *Sisyrinchium bellum* IRIS FAMILY
6 petals forming this star-shaped flower. It has grass or rush-like, single, pointed leaves. They stand clustered in bunches. Blooms in late March to early April.

Blue-eyed Marys/Chinese Pagodas *Collinsia sp.* SNAPDRAGON FAMILY
5 petals united to form 2 lips, an upper and a lower. The heads of flowers are in tiered clusters, the upper petals being white and the lower blue. Blooms in March and April.

Brodiaea *Brodiaea sp.* LILY FAMILY
6 long and thin petals, that are united at the base. Single tall, bare flower stalk up to 2 feet high topped with a cluster of a few flowers. Pale to dark purple. Pronounced "brody-uh." Blooms in April.

Grass Widows *Sisyrinchium douglasii* IRIS FAMILY
6 petals forming this star-shaped flower. It has grass or rush-like, single, pointed leaves. Stands clustered in bunches. Blooms in March.

Larkspur *Delphinium menziesii* BUTTERCUP FAMILY
5 petals, each flower having a large spur protruding from its back. Usually has 4 or more flowers at the top. All plant parts are hairy, the leaves parsley-like. Blooms in mid to late April.

Lupine *Lupinus sp.* PEA FAMILY
Pea-like flowers, mostly blue with white. Usually found on mounds, this plant is very common. Distinctive fan-like leaves and pea-pod fruit. Blooms in April and May.

Penstemon *Penstemon sp.* SNAPDRAGON FAMILY
5 petals, 2 upward angled lips and 3 downward lower lobes. Tubular flowers on 1/2–3 foot stems, blue with white throat. Blooms in May through July.

Poverty Clover/Cow's Udder *Trifolium depauperatum* PEA FAMILY
Small, low-lying plants with tiny, puffed, purple to magenta flowers shaped like upturned cow's udders. Common on tops of The Rocks in depressions. Blooms in April.

Shooting Star *Dodecatheon hendersonii* PRIMROSE FAMILY
5 petals. Has a whorl of basal leaves. The nodding flowers are atop a leaf-less stalk. The petals are flared back from a black center. Blooms in April.

Vetch *Vicia villosa* PEA FAMILY
Long racemes or rows of crowded pea-like flowers, purple to magenta. This is a climbing plant with coiling tendrils and soft hairs. Very common on the hillsides of the valley, it is a valued green fodder and adds nitrogen to the soil. Introduced from Europe. Blooms May through July.

EE

FF

GG

HH

II

JJ

KK

BLUE AND PURPLE FLOWERS

EE—Blue-eyed Grass *Sisyrinchium bellum*; FF—Blue-eyed Mary/Chinese Pagodas *Collinsia sp.*; GG—Downingia *Downingia yina*; HH—Hound's Tongue *Cynoglossum grande*; II—Miniature Lupine *Lupinus bicolor*; JJ—Penstemon *Penstemon sp.*; KK—Mound Flora—April, Lower Table Rock.

LL

MM

NN

OO

PP

QQ

BLUE AND PURPLE FLOWERS (Cont'd.)

LL—Camas *Camassia leichtlinii*; MM—Cat's Ear *Calochortus tolmiei*;
NN—Common Brodiaea *Brodiaea sp.*; OO—Elegant Brodiaea *Brodiaea elegans*;
PP—Larkspur *Delphinium menziesii*; QQ—Tissue Flower (Rare) *Toiletpapyrus sp.*

❦ BLUE/PURPLE FLOWERS (Cont'd.)

Woodland

Naked Broomrape *Orobanche uniflora* Broomrape Family
Dark purple to bluish to yellow tubular, nodding flower on a single 3–5 inch stem. Lacks green leaves as it is parasitic on other plants! Blooms in April.

Hound's Tongue *Cynoglossum grande* Borage Family
5 petals, the blue flower having a center of white. This plant has large green leaves at its base with a stalk arising from the middle and many flowers along its length. Blooms in early April.

Larkspur *Delphinium menziesii* Buttercup Family
5 petals, each flower having a large spur protruding from its back. Usually has 4 or more flowers at the top. All plant parts are hairy, the leaves parsley-like. Blooms in mid to late April.

Mission Bell *Fritillaria lanceolata* Lily Family
6 petal-like segments and nodding flower. Brownish-purple mottled with greenish-yellow spots. Narrow leaves on upper part of a 1–4'stem. Blooms in February.

Poverty Clover/Cow's Udder *Trifolium depauperatum* Pea Family
Small, low-lying plants with tiny, puffed, purple to magenta flowers shaped like upturned cow's udders. Common on tops of The Rocks in depressions. Blooms in April.

Shooting Star *Dodecatheon hendersonii* Primrose Family
5 petals. Has a whorl of basal leaves. The nodding flowers are atop a leafless stalk. The petals are flared back from a black center. Blooms in April.

Chaparral

Camas *Camassia leichtlinii* Lily Family
6 petals. This plant has a large spike of flowers that open from the bottom up. Common along the trail in the wetter areas. Its bulb was a Takelma food staple. Blooms from late April into May.

Brodiaea *Brodiaea sp.* Lily Family
6 long and thin petals, that are united at the base. Single tall, bare flower stalk up to 2 feet high topped with a cluster of a few flowers. Pale to dark purple. Pronounced "brody-uh." Blooms in April.

Shooting Star *Dodecatheon hendersonii* Primrose Family
5 petals. Has a whorl of basal leaves. The nodding flowers are atop a leafless stalk. The petals are flared back from a black center. Blooms in April.

Rock/Scabland

Grass Widows *Sisyrinchium douglasii* Iris Family
6 petals forming this star-shaped flower. It has grass or rush-like, single, pointed leaves. Stands clustered in bunches. Blooms in March.

Poverty Clover/Cow's Udder *Trifolium depauperatum* PEA FAMILY
Small, low-lying plants with tiny, puffed, purple to magenta flowers shaped like upturned cow's udders. Common on tops of The Rocks in depressions. Blooms in April.

Pool/Wet Areas

Baby Blue Eyes *Nemophila pedunculata* WATERLEAF FAMILY
5 petals and opposite leaves. Low and slightly succulent, its usually found on gopher mounds. Blooms in April.

Camas *Camassia leichtlinii* LILY FAMILY
6 petals. This plant has a large spike of flowers that open from the bottom up. Common along the trail in the wetter areas. Its bulb was a Takelma food staple. Blooms from late April into May.

Downingia *Downingia yina* BLUEBELL FAMILY
5 petals, 3 larger bottom ones united, the top two free and smaller. Has a yellow spot in the center. This small plant (less than 6 inches) often carpets pool bottoms. Blooms in late April and May.

Additional Flower Chart

There is a flower chart available from the publisher that contains more flowering plants than the Flower Guide has room for. While it does not contain descriptive accounts of the flowers, it does make a check list for the less common plants you may see. It is approximately thirty pages, arranged in flower colors, and will be sent photocopied on 8-1/2" x 11" paper. The cost is $5.00. If interested, send your remittance to:

Last Minute Publications

Phone#(541)-535-7659

Sorry, it is a toll call.

APPENDIX A

Takelma Language

Place Names[1]

'Alwiya....................Roxy Ann Peak.
Dilomi:......................"West of which are cedars" large Upland Takelma
                            village upriver from town of Gold Hill.
Lat-gau:....................Upland Takelma village thought to have been
                            between Talent and Ashland, its other name,
                            La-waya meaning "knife in belly."
Lath'kawkh:..............."Front of person"—Grizzly Peak.
Ma-lsi:....................Mt. McLoughlin.
Sa'thkawkh:...............Bear Creek Valley—"the whole plain from Table
                            Rock to Ashland."
Si-ku-ptat:..............."Dirty water"—Bear Creek.
Titanakh:................."Little Indian plums"—Table Rock.
Di'tani:..................."Rock above"—Table Rock.
Tats'ipe-kwankh:..........Derived from ts'ipiks or grasshopper—
                            The Agate Desert.
Ti'lo-mi-kh:..............a waterfall or rapids upriver from the town of
                            Gold Hill. Location of the Story Rock.

Takelma Stories

The Rainmaker[2]

A stout man named Khu-khu-w came from the east to Table Rock. The Rogue River was so low the local Indians could not catch salmon. The Table Rock Indians hired Khu-khu-w to make rain. At first, they tried to swap blankets, offering him a soft one. His own blanket was so rough and sharp, it made a noise when one handled it. He turned them down, saying "soft blanket no good, rough blanket warm blanket!"

He said he could make a little water, but he couldn't stop it! It flooded all this lowland, and Gold Hill only stuck out a little! He drowned lots of Indians. Because the survivors were out to kill him, Khu-khu-w took his family and escaped to the top of Table Rock. His son, daughter-in-law, and their little son turned to rock and are the pinnacles seen at the west tip of Table Rock. Khu-khu-w himself turned into a good sized cedar!

Boy Turned to Cedar[3]

A boy cried for more grub all the time, so they put him in a sack and put him outdoors. Thkwala, a big horned owl, stole the baby and put him on top of Table Rock. He cried, "Oh, come after me, papa!" They hired Beaver to get that baby, but before he could get to him, the boy had turned to cedar.

Daldal Saves The People[4]

Daldal, giant dragonfly, dwelt in a house by the sea. One day, he saw dismembered bodies of people floating down the river. Concerned with the great numbers of bodies, he decided to travel upriver to find out what was happening.

Along the way, he saw a lark flying overhead. He shot an arrow up and it went right through Lark's nose! The arrow came back down and struck Daldal between his eyes. It split him completely in two, so now he had a younger brother. Younger Daldal agreed to travel upriver with him. Someone told them that people were being destroyed at Dilomi.

Elder Daldal was quiet and graceful, leading the way up river. Younger Daldal tripped along behind, asking all sorts of questions, and getting his nose into trouble.

They had to wrestle their way upstream, tangling with black and white oaks, firs, berry bushes, all sorts of things! They became very strong.

Along the way, the younger Daldal traded some shell money for a certain special shell. His aunt, Bluejay, was reluctant to sell the shell because it belonged to her son, K'uk'u, the wild man of the woods. Sure enough, when K'uk'u found out, he caught up with the young dragonfly and challenged him to fight. The youngster hid in a tree and cried, "O elder brother!" Daldal the elder transformed K'uk'u into the Echo.

Next, they met an old man running from a house in the woods. He was an evil being who could turn himself into blood. The younger dragonfly fell for this trick and ate him. As he was choking to death, he gasped, "O elder brother!" Daldal stuck a flint-flaker down his throat to save him. The elder Daldal scolded his younger brother, "Let it alone!"

Back on their way, they came upon a warm house. An old woman invited them in, saying "Warrrm your back!" The elder Daldal ignored the offer, but the kid, of course, went in. He taunted, "Big-nosed Daldal, put on style! You just stand there. I'm going in!" The old woman tried to push the little brother into the fire. "O elder brother!", he screamed. Once again, elder Daldal rescued him, and then turned the woman into a certain bush of the swamps. "Food you will be," he told her.

Travelling a little further, they came upon two blind women, without any eyes at all. They were sitting together pounding tarweed seeds. The younger dragonfly teased them, stealing their flour and tying their long hair together. Each thinking it was the other woman who was doing this, the two got into a fistfight. The young Daldal was watching from the roof, laughing! He called to his brother, "Big-nosed Daldal!" The women stopped fighting, saying, "So it was he that did it!" To set things right, elder Daldal made each of them a pair of eyes, using a pointed stick heated in the fire.

And so they went, meeting more challenges. Elder Daldal transformed evil beings into useful things: mussels, sinew for arrows, salmon-spears. They found homes deserted, with nothing but household implements in them. It seemed evil beings possessed the tools, killing their owners.

At last they came upon the village Dilomi. It was controlled by two wicked men, who were presently fishing for salmon. The Daldals challenged them to a wrestling match, and everyone from the village watched. After a tough battle, they slew the two wicked ones. Daldal the elder threw the older man's body into the air, toward the west, saying "The Evening Star you shall always be called!" He did the same with the younger man, throwing his body to the east to become the morning star.

Coyote snatched up the fishing net the wicked men had dropped and tried to catch himself some salmon. On the first throw, he caught only mice! The second, he caught only gophers! Daldal explained that Coyote must hunt in the earth.

Daldal blessed the people from Dilomi, in front of the falls. He said, "People shall spear salmon, they will go to get food, to one another they will go to get food. One another they will feed. They shall not kill one another! In that way shall the world be, as long as the world goes on." Right there salmon are always caught in the nets.

The brothers went on a little ways more, the elder one ahead. The elder brother whistled and they turned into mountains! The elder one was short, the younger one was long. Nowadays they are standing there! Younger Daldal is Lower Table Rock and Elder Daldal is called Upper Table Rock!

Medicine Formulas[5]
When Yellowhammer Talks: "Didst thou discover people are coming?"

When new moon appears: "I shall prosper, I shall yet remain alive. Even if people say of me, 'Would that he died!', just like thee I shall do, again shall I arise...when frogs eat thee up,...lizards...still dost thou rise again. Just like thee shall I do in time to come."

When one sneezes: "Who calls my name? 'Thou shalt prosper,'shall ye say of me, 'yet another day mayest thou continue to live.' Ye shall blow (a whiff of tobacco smoke) to me."

A prayer to the wind: "He! From down my body shalt thou drive out evil things, from the crown of my head shalt thou drive them out, from over my hands shalt thou drive them out, from within my backbone shalt thou drive out evil things."

---

[1]Gray, Dennis J., *The Takelma and Their Athapascan Neighbors*, 1987.
[2]Gray, Dennis J., *The Takelma and Their Athapascan Neighbors,* 1987. Title by Dennis Gray. Minor variations by editor.
[3]Gray, Dennis J., *The Takelma and Their Athapascan Neighbors*, 1987. Title by Dennis Gray. Minor variations by editor.
[4]Sapir, Edward, *Takelma Texts*, 1909. Title and Interpretation by editor, with help from Thomas Doty.
[5]Sapir, Edward, *Takelma Texts*, 1909. Minor variations by editor.

For more local Indian stories, check out *Mythtime Writings, Volume 1-5*, by Thomas Doty. Available at Jackson County Libraries.

APPENDIX B

TREATY WITH THE ROGUE RIVER, 1853.

TREATY WITH THE ROGUE RIVER, 1853.

Whereas a treaty was made and entered into at Table Rock, near Rogue River, in the Territory of Oregon, this 10th day of September, A. D. 1853, by and between Joel Palmer, superintendent of Indian affairs, and Samuel H. Culver, Indian agent, on the part of the United States; and Jo-aps-er-ka-har, principal chief, Sam To-qua-he-ar, and Jim Ana-cha-a-rah, subordinate chiefs, and others, head-men of the bands of the Rogue River tribe of Indians, on the part of said tribe.

Sept. 10, 1853.
10 Stats., 1018.
Ratified Apr. 12, 1854.
Proclaimed Feb. 5, 1855.

ARTICLE 1. The Rogue River tribe of Indians do hereby cede and relinquish, for the considerations hereinafter specified, to the United States, all their right, title, interest, and claim to all the lands lying in that part of the Territory of Oregon, and bounded by lines designated as follows, to wit: .

Cession of lands in Oregon.

Commencing at a point one mile below the mouth of Applegate Creek, on the south side of Rogue River, running thence southerly to the highlands dividing the waters of Applegate Creek from those of Althouse Creek, thence along said highlands to the summit of the Siskiyon range of mountains, thence easterly to Pilot Rock, thence northeasterly to the summit of the Cascade range, thence northerly along the said Cascade range to Pitt's Peak, continuing northerly to Rogue River, thence westerly to the head-waters of Jump-off-jo Creek, thence down said creek to the intersection of the same with a line due north from the place of beginning, thence to the place of beginning.

ARTICLE 2. It is agreed on the part of the United States that the aforesaid tribe shall be allowed to occupy temporarily that portion of the above-described tract of territory bounded as follows, to wit: Commencing on the north side of Rogue River, at the mouth of Evan's Creek; thence up said creek to the upper end of a small prairie bearing in a northwesterly direction from Table Mountain, or Upper Table Rock, thence through the gap to the south side of the cliff of the said mountain, thence in a line to Rogue River, striking the southern base of Lower Table Rock, thence down said river to the place of beginning. It being understood that this described tract of land shall be deemed and considered an Indian reserve, until a suitable selection shall be made by the direction of the President of the United States for their permanent residence and buildings erected thereon, and provision made for their removal.

Indians to occupy a portion of the ceded land temporarily.

Permanent home to be selected.

ARTICLE 3. For and in consideration of the cession and relinquishment contained in article 1st, the United States agree to pay to the aforesaid tribe the sum of sixty thousand dollars, fifteen thousand of which sum to be retained, (according to the stipulations of article 4th of a "treaty of peace made and entered into on the 8th day of September, 1853,[a] between Gen'l Jo. Lane, commanding forces of Oregon Territory, and Jo., principal chief, Sam and Jim, subordinate chiefs, on the part of the Rogue River tribe of Indians,") by the superintendent of Indian affairs, to pay for the property of the whites destroyed by them during the late war, the amount of property so destroyed to be estimated by three disinterested commissioners, to be appointed by the superintendent of Indian affairs, or otherwise, as the President may direct. Five thousand dollars to be expended in the purchase of agricultural implements, blankets, clothing, and such other goods as may be deemed by the superintendent, or agent most conducive to the comfort and necessities of said tribe, on or before the 1st day of September, 1854; and for the payment of such permanent improvements as may have been made by land claimants on the aforesaid reserve, the

Payment for said cession.

---

[a] This agreement is unratified and a copy of the original agreement on file in the Indian Office (Oregon, 1844–1858, Ore. Sup. L., 323) has been included in the Appendix, post, p. 1049.

TREATY WITH THE ROGUE RIVER, 1853.

value of which to be ascertained by three persons appointed by the said superintendent.

The remaining forty thousand dollars to be paid in sixteen equal annual instalments, of two thousand five hundred dollars each, (commencing on or about the 1st day of September, 1854,) in blankets, clothing, farming-utensils, stock, and such other articles as may be deemed most conducive to the interests of said tribe.

Buildings to be erected. ARTICLE 4. It is further agreed that there shall be erected, at the expense of the United States, one dwelling-house for each of the three principal chiefs of the aforesaid tribe, the cost of which shall not exceed five hundred dollars each, the aforesaid buildings to be erected as soon after the ratification of this treaty as possible. And when the tribe may be removed to another reserve, buildings and other improvements shall be made on such reserve of equal value to those which *Additional payments on removal.* may be relinquished; and upon such removal, in addition to the beforementioned sixty thousand dollars, the United States agree to pay the further sum of fifteen thousand dollars, in five equal annual instalments, commencing at the expiration of the before-named instalments.

Protection of travelers. ARTICLE 5. The said tribe of Indians further agree to give safe-conduct to all persons who may be authorized to pass through their reserve, and to protect, in their person and property, all agents or other persons sent by the United States to reside among them; they further agree not to molest or interrupt any white person passing through their reserve.

Redress for individual grievances. ARTICLE 6. That the friendship which is now established between the United States and the Rogue River tribe of Indians shall not be interrupted by the misconduct of individuals, it is hereby agreed that for injuries done by individuals no private revenge or retaliation shall take place; but instead thereof, complaint shall be made by the party injured to the Indian agent; and it shall be the duty of the chiefs of the said tribe, that upon complaint being made as aforesaid, to deliver up the person or persons against whom the complaint is made, to the end that he or they may be punished agreeably to the laws of the United States; and in like manner if any violation, robbery, or murder shall be committed on any Indian or Indians belonging to said tribe, the person or persons so offending shall be tried, and if found guilty, shall be punished according to the laws of the United States. *Restitution of stolen property.* And it is agreed that the chiefs of the said tribe shall, to the utmost of their power, exert themselves to recover horses or other property, which has or may be stolen or taken from any citizen or citizens of the United States, by any individual of said tribe; and the property so recovered shall be forthwith delivered to the Indian agent or other person authorized to receive the same, that it may be restored to the proper owner.

Guaranty for property stolen from Indians. And the United States hereby guarantee to any Indian or Indians of the said tribe a full indemnification for any horses or other property which may be stolen from them by any citizens of the United States: *Provided,* That the property stolen or taken cannot be recovered, and that sufficient proof is produced that it was actually stolen or taken by a citizen of the United States. And the chiefs and head-men of the said tribe engage, on the requisition or demand of the President of the United States, superintendent of Indian affairs, or Indian agent, to deliver up any white person or persons resident among them.

Farms may be established. ARTICLE 7. It is agreed between the United States and the Rogue River tribe of Indians, that, should it at any time hereafter be considered by the United States as a proper policy to establish farms among and for the benefit of said Indians, it shall be discretionary with the President, by and with the advice and consent of the Senate, to change the annuities herein provided for, or any part thereof, into a fund for that purpose.

TREATY WITH THE ROGUE RIVER, 1853.

ARTICLE 8. This treaty shall take effect and be obligatory on the contracting parties as soon as the same shall have been ratified by the President of the United States by and with the advice and consent of the Senate.

In testimony whereof the said Joel Palmer and Samuel H. Culver, on the part of the United States, and the chiefs and headmen of the Rogue River Indians aforesaid, have hereunto set their hands and seals, the day and year aforesaid.

Joel Palmer,	[L. S.]
Superintendent Indian Affairs.	
Samuel H. Culver,	[L. S.]
Indian Agent.	
Jo, his x mark,	[L. S.]
Aps-er-ka-har,	
Sam, his x mark,	[L. S.]
To-qua-he-ar,	
Jim, his x mark,	[L. S.]
Ana-chah-a-rah,	
John, his x mark,	[L. S.]
Lympe, his x mark,	[L. S.]

Signed in presence of—
  J. W. Nesmith, Interpreter,
  R. B. Metcalf,
  John, his x mark,
  J. D. Mason, Secretary,
  T. T. Tierney.
Witness,
  Joseph Lane,
  August V. Kautz.

We the undersigned principal chief, subordinate chiefs and headmen of the bands of the Rogue River tribe of Indians, parties to the treaty concluded at Table Rock, near Rogue River, in the Territory of Oregon, on the 10th day of September, A. D. 1853, having had fully explained to us the amendment made to the same by the Senate of the United States, on the 12th day of April, 1854, do hereby accept and consent to the said amendment to the treaty aforesaid, and agree that the same shall be considered as a part thereof.

In testimony whereof we have hereunto set our hands and affixed our seals, this 11th day of November, A. D. 1854.

Aps-so-ka-hah, Horse-rider, or Jo, his x mark.	[L. S.]
Ko-ko-ha-wah, Wealthy, or Sam, his x mark.	[L. S.]
Te-cum-tom, Elk Killer, or John, his x mark.	[L. S.]
Chol-cul-tah, Joquah Trader, or George, his x mark.	[L. S.]

Executed in presence of—
  Edward H. Geary, Secretary
  Cris. Taylor,
  John Flett,
  R. B. Metcalf, Interpreter,
  Joel Palmer, Superintendent.

APPENDIX C

MT photos by Bert Fox

Top of the rock

LOWER TABLE ROCK — After long and continuing efforts to preserve Lower Table Rock and Kelly Slough as natural areas, officials of the Nature Conservancy Friday dedicated a plaque to commemorate a significant source of financial assistance.

Spencer Beebe, Northwest director of the Nature Conservancy from Portland, puts the finishing touches on the mount for the plaque, below. It is situated about one-third of way along lip of rock from left in top photo.

The plaque memorializes the late Elmer Feldenheimer, a Jackson County orchardist who owned property near the rock. He had been fond of hiking on and around the rock.

After his death, his sister Marie Louise established the revolving Elmer Feldenheimer Land Preservation Fund for use in Northwest conservation projects. The Nature Conservancy borrowed money from the fund to finance the initial purchase of 750 acres of the rock. Donations are repaying the loan and for a conservation easement of 900 acres obtained from landowner George Neary.

The rock is site of several rare plants and one of the most diverse wildflower blooms in the Northwest. Kelley Slough, the placid backwaters of Gold Ray Dam on the Rogue River, part of which is seen in photo at right, harbors a variety of wildlife, most notably one of the largest blue heron rookeries in the state.

129

A The MAIL TRIBUNE, Medford, Oregon, Monday, September 21, 1981

TABLE ROCK DIST.

Lifestyles

Medford
sportsman led
this reporter on

A hike into history

By DICK JEWETT
Mail Tribune Senior Staff Writer

A climb up the extremely steep slopes below the south-facing stone bluffs of Lower Table Rock on a scorching September day generates nothing but respect for 11 men who made the same climb 128 years ago.

A mixture of stickery grass, brush, live and fallen trees and large rocks cover the hillside. Deer trails provide some access in the ascent, but frequent bushwhacking is required. The last part of the exhausting climb to a shelf below the cliff is hazardous — over large, loose lava boulders.

For the soldiers and civilians, led by Gen. Joseph Lane on Sept. 10, 1853, the ascent was no ordinary recreation outing. It was business with danger far greater than a loose rock or a misstep on the hillside.

The men had left their firearms behind and were bound for an armed camp of hostile Rogue River Indians to negotiate a peace treaty following an armistice. For all they knew, they were inviting death.

Medford sportsman John Day, a history buff, led the way last Sunday to the approximate spot of the Council of Table Rock where an agreement was signed that restored peace for the next two years. Day, former owner of the property now held by the Nature Conservancy, says the location was pointed out to him years ago by John Edgar Ross, son of Col. John E. Ross, a member of Lane's party.

A marker placed along Table Rock Road in 1928 by the Daughters of the American Revolution says the treaty was signed "near this spot." The site shown by Day is about two miles south and west of the marker.

Day says he is hesitant that he might offend the women of the DAR with his identification of the place. But he says, "I wanted to pinpoint the site before it is lost in history."

Day spent weeks of checking with historical society officials and Ross family members for information on the signing before taking this Mail Tribune reporter to the site.

Among the material he gathered is "A reminiscence of the Indian War, 1853," by Capt. James W. Nesmith, who served as interpreter for Lane on the treaty mission and was later a U.S. senator from Oregon.

In the journal, Nesmith said the armistice had followed a fight in the Evans Creek area in which the Indians apparently got the worst of it.

Nesmith told how Lane's troops camped along the river prior to negotiations while "the Indians selected a strong and almost inaccessible position, high up, and just under the perpendicular cliffs of Table Rock." The groups awaited the arrival of Gen. Joel Palmer, superintendent of Indian Affairs for Oregon, and Samuel P. Culver, Indian agent, before beginning the parley.

"At night we could plainly see their (the Indians') campfire," while they could look directly down upon us," Nesmith wrote.

"On the morning of that day (Sept. 10)," said Nesmith, "General Lane sent for me, and desired me to go with him to the council ground inside the Indian encampment, to act as interpreter, as I was

MT photo by Dick Jewett

John Day leads the way to the location of the "Council of Table Rock"

a master of the Chinook jargon. Nesmith said he protested going into the camp because he had fought the same Indians before, they were "notoriously treacherous" and it was "criminal folly."

But he told Lane that he would accompany him "to what I believed would be our slaughter."

"After riding a couple of miles across the level valley, we came to the foot of the mountain where it was too steep for horses to ascend," Nesmith said. "We dismounted and hitched our horses and scrambled for half a mile over huge rocks and through brush, and then found ourselves in the Indian stronghold, just under the perpendicular cliff of Table Rock, surrounded by 700 fierce and well-armed savages, in all their gorgeous war paint and feathers."

"It was a bright and beautiful morning," Nesmith wrote. "The Rogue River Valley lay like a panorama at our feet." He said the line of mounted soldiers below "looked like they were engraven on a picture."

Nesmith also told that the shooting of an Indian by white men was reported during the parley, almost breaking it up and endangering the white negotiators.

He said Lane calmed the Indians down by promising to punish the leader of those responsible for the killing and agreeing to give fair compensation for the dead man in shirts and blankets.

Nesmith said after the 11 men went back down the hill and rode across the valley, "I drew a long breath and remarked to the old General that the next time he wanted to go unarmed into a hostile camp he must hunt up someone besides myself to act as interpreter."

Among the information rounded up by Day is a letter written in 1879 by Lane commending Nesmith and saying, "Dates and incidents given in the article are in the main correct."

Lane said "the Rogue's, proper, never forgot the impression we made upon them in the great council of Sept. 10, 1853. It was a grand and successful council. The Rogue Rivers, proper, fought us no more; they did not forget their promise to us."

The bench area on which Day says the treaty was negotiated is not accessible to the public since it is on private land well off the beaten track.

The complete list of the men who braved the Indian camp:

Gen. Joseph Lane, Gen. Joel Palmer, Samuel P. Culver, Capt. A.J. Smith, Capt. L.F. Mosher, Col. John E. Ross, Capt. J.W. Nesmith, Lt. A.V. Kautz, R.B. Metcalf, J.D. Mason, T.T. Tierney.

The *Mail Tribune*, Medford, Oregon. September 21, 1981.

APPENDIX E

Legend of the Table Rock Leper
Abridged from the *Mail Tribune* Article by Dale Vincent—December 7, 1947

Jacksonville Leper Left Legend of Gold Discovery in Vicinity of Table Rock

In the gold rush days of the 50's, Jacksonville was a booming gold town. People had gathered here from every part of the world. There were few countries that were not represented by at least a few of that nationality.

There were Swedes, French, Spanish, Irish, English, and of course, the Indian and ever-present John Chinaman.

All of these were rugged, strong characters, but one day there appeared among them—a leper.

When this was discovered by a few of the good citizens, they were filled with horror and alarm. What should they do with this scourge that had come among them?

They desired, of course, to be rid of the leper, but the victim was still a human being, and therefore must be dealt with in a sympathetic and humane manner.

So these few good citizens held a secret meeting—not wanting to spread any alarm—yet determined to safeguard their community.

Taken to Cabin

At last they hit upon a plan. Appropriations were made for expenses, and a committee of three was elected to escort the leper out of town, across Rogue River, and to the inside bend of the horseshoe that was formed by the Table Rocks.

At the base of one of the cliffs, they built a cabin and stocked it with groceries. The grateful leper promised to live there in isolation.

The purpose of the committee from then on was to purchase food and clothing and take it to the leper once a month.

These supplies were delivered in an odd manner. The committee, riding horseback and leading a pack mule, would ascend to the top of the Table Rock cliffs, just above the cabin. From that point they would lower down to the waiting leper, a wooden bucket filled with supplies, on the end of a rope.

This unique grocery delivery service was kept up regularly every month for a period of more than two years.

Leper Acts Queer

Then one day in the spring of the third year the bucket was let... down as usual and the committee...could see the small figure of a man far below come feebly out of his cabin and make his way slowly to the base of the cliff where the bucket rested.

The leper acted as though he might be unusually sick. But finally the bucket was unloaded of its food and a feeble tug on the rope was given as a signal to raise the bucket.

But the men at the top found the bucket very heavy and thinking it was still loaded with food, they waited. The signal came again...The men pulled on the rope once more. It was still heavy.

What could be wrong? Had the leper climbed into the bucket, the men wondered, in hope they would pull him to the top?

They snubbed the rope to a tree and one of them peeked over the edge of the cliff. The leper was going back to his cabin and the bucket looked as empty as ever.

The committee could not imagine what made the bucket so heavy, but they struggled and lifted and sweat until they got it to the top.

Gold in Bucket

Their amazement was profound. The bottom of the bucket was filled four inches deep with gold nuggets and dust.

This then was their reward from the grateful leper, for all the years they had carried him food. But where had he got the gold?

The men hurried back to Jacksonville and shared the reward with the rest of the few citizens who knew about the leper and who had been contributing to his welfare. All wondered if the leper had discovered a rich mine near his cabin—but no one was willing to go near the leper to look.

On their next trip the committee lowered their provisions as usual, but this time no one came to receive them. The cabin was silent and there was no movement anywhere. Apparently the leper had died.

To this day no explanation has ever been found as to where that gold came from.

Did the old man have a rich mine at the base of the Table Rocks? Or had he just cleaned out a pocket?

Old River Channel

It has been said that no gold to speak of has ever been found around the lava formations of the Table Rocks. But one mining engineer, now living in the valley, thinks it possible that one of the old, prehistoric river channels (that are noted for their heavy gold content) runs close to the base of the Rocks and has been covered over by the more recent flow of lava that formed the Table Rocks.

It could be possible that the old leper somehow tapped this old river channel. We do not know.

The above lost mine story cannot be authenticated in any way. It is a legend that has been handed down by word-of-mouth from one old-timer to another.

APPENDIX F

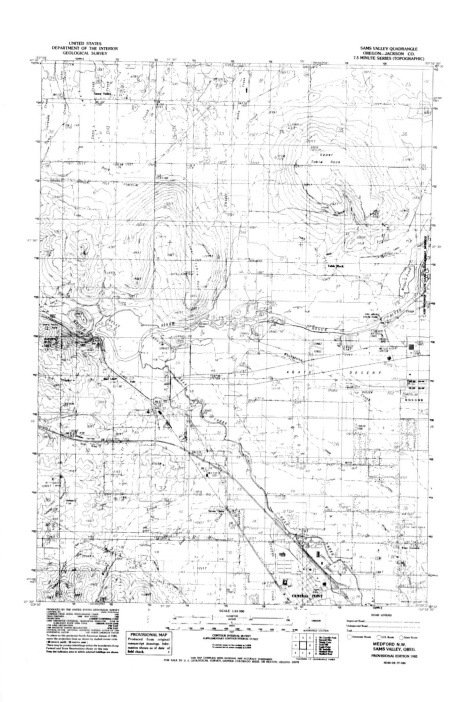

ANNOTATED BIBLIOGRAPHY

Arno, Stephen F. *Northwest Trees*, The Mountaineers, Seattle, WA, 1977.

Beckham, Stephen Dow. *Requiem for a People: The Rogue Indians and the Frontiersman*, University of Oklahoma Press, Norman, OK, 1971.

———. *The Indians of Western Oregon: This Land Was Theirs*, Arago Books, Coos Bay, OR, 1977.

Beeson, John. *A Plea For The Indians*, Ye Galleon Press, Fairfield, WA, Reprint 1982.

Bernstein, Art. *Native Trees of the Northwest: A Pocket Guide*, New Leaf Books, Grants Pass, OR, 1988.

Bondinell, Carl. "The Continuing History of Jackson County," A 13-Part Special Supplement to The Morning News:
Part 2, "The Indians" March 3, 1979.
Part 3, "The White Man Comes 1826-1848."
Part 4, "Gold miners, Jacksonville and the first war with the Indians."
Part 5, "1853: through the eyes of a pioneer woman."
Part 6, "The final Indian wars in the Rogue Valley."

Booth, Percy T. *Valley of the Rogues*, Josephine County Historical Society, Grants Pass, OR, 1970.

Borgias, Darren. "Table Rock Interpretive Program Docent Training Guide," Unpublished. 1979 and 1992.

———. Personal Communication, 1991-93. Preserve Manager for The Nature Conservancy.

Bork, Joyce Lynn. "A Survey of the Vascular Plants and Vertebrates of Upper Table Rock." Unpublished Master's thesis. Southern Oregon State College, Ashland, OR, 1978.

Buan, Carolyn and Richard Lewis. *The First Oregonians*. Oregon Council for the Humanities, Portland, OR, 1991.

Card, Virginia D. "The Takelma Indians of Southwestern Oregon (Now Extinct)," unpublished manuscript, 1967.

Casilio, Don. "Know Your Trees." US Forest Service booklet assembled by the Ashland Ranger District from articles that appeared in the *Medford Mail Tribune*, January 23-March 13, 1989.

Chipman, Art. *Wildflower Trails of the Pacific Northwest*, Pine Cone Publishers, Medford, OR, 1970.

Clark, Lewis J. *Wild Flowers of the Pacific Northwest*, Gray's Publishing Limited. Sidney, BC, Canada, 1976.

Doty, Thomas. *Mythtime Writings:*
Volume 1: Making the World
Volume 2: Sometimes the Sun and Moon Travel Together
Volume 3: In the Forest, By the River
Volume 4: Coyote Makes Tracks All Over The World Ashland, OR, 1985.

———. Personal Communication, 1993. Has led interpretive hikes for TNC/BLM.

Engeman, Richard H. "The Jacksonville Story," Table Rock Sentinel Sept./Oct. 1990.

Francis, Mary Evans. *The Book of Grasses*, Doubleday, Page and Co., Garden City, NY, 1920.

Gilkey, Helen M. and La Rea J. Dennis. *Handbook of Northwestern Plants*. Oregon State University Bookstores, Inc., Corvallis, OR, 1967.

Gray, Dennis J. "The Takelma and Their Athapascan Neighbors," *University of Oregon Anthropological Papers No. 37*, University of Oregon, Eugene, OR, 1987.

Hannon, Nan and Richard Olmo. *Living With the Land: The Indians of Southwest Oregon.* Southern Oregon Historical Society, Medford, OR, 1990.

Hawkins, Bob. Personal Communication, 1993. Involved in initial preservation activities and leader of TR hikes for church and Scout groups for 15 years.

Hitchcock, A.S. *Manual of the Grasses of the United States*, United States Government Printing Office, Washington, DC, 1951.

Hitchcock, C. Leo and Arthur Cronquist. *Flora of the Pacific Northwest*, University of Washington Press, Seattle, WA, 1973.

Horn, Elizabeth L. *Wildflowers 1—The Cascades*, The Touchstone Press, Beaverton, OR, 1972.

Ifft, John. Personal Communication, 1991. Retired Planner for the Bureau of Land Management, past member of the Lower Table Rock Stewardship Committee, and participant in building the Table Rock trails.

Jackman, Andrew and Art Bernstein. *The Hip-Pocket Naturalist A Guide to Oregon's Rogue River Basin.*, Magnifica Books, Grants Pass, OR, 1989.

Jepson, Willis Linn. *A Manual of the Flowering Plants of California*, Associated Students Store, University of California, Berkeley, CA, 1925.

Kasner, Leone Letson. *Siletz: Survival For An Artifact*, Itemizer-Observer, Dallas, OR, 1977.

Kent, William Eugene. *The Siletz Indian Reservation 1855-1900*, Lincoln County Historical Society, Newport, OR, 1977.

Kinney, Harold. Personal Communication, 1993. Member of Experimental Aircraft Owners Association.

Kramer, George. *Camp White: City in the Agate Desert*, Camp White 50th Anniversary Committee, White City, OR, 1992.

Kranz, Ronald and John Richter. "Lower Table Rock Preserve-A Stewardship Master Plan," Unpublished report prepared for the Oregon Chapter of The Nature Conservancy, 1980.

Kritzman, Ellen B. *Little Mammals of the Pacific Northwest.* Pacific Search Press, Seattle, WA, 1977.

LaLande, Jeff. *First Over The Siskiyous*, Historical Society Press, Portland, OR, 1987.

———. Personal communication, 1993.

Latimer, Shane. "Table Rock Flower Guide," Unpublished report for internship with The Nature Conservancy, 1990.

Leviton, Alan E. *Reptiles and Amphibians of North America.* Doubleday & Company, Inc., New York, NY.

McArthur, Lewis A. *Oregon Geographic Names*, Oregon Historical Society Press, Portland, OR, 1992.

McMinn, Howard E. *An Illustrated Manual of California Shrubs.* University of California Press, Berkeley, CA, 1964.

Niehaus, Theodore F. and Charles L. Ripper. *A Field Guide to Pacific States Wildflowers*, Houghton Mifflin Co., Boston, MA, 1976.

O'Harra, Marjorie. *Southern Oregon: Short Trips Into History*, Southern Oregon Historical Society, Jacksonville, OR, 1985.

———. "Drive-along History," Table Rock Sentinel May/June 1991.

Oregon Society of the Daughters of the American Revolution, *Oregon Historical Landmarks: Southern Oregon*, The Drain Enterprise, Drain, OR, 1974.

Peck, Morton E. *A Manual of the Higher Plants of Oregon*, Binfords and Mort, Portland, OR, 1941.

Pilgrim, Agnes. Personal Communication, 1992. Descendant of Takelma Indians.

Randall, Warren R., Robert F. Keniston, Dale N. Bever, and Edward C. Jensen. *Manual of Oregon Trees and Shrubs.* OSU Bookstores, Inc., Corvallis, OR, 1981.

Ray, Susan. "Snowbound for a Day," Table Rock Sentinel March/April 1990.

Robison, Houston T., *The Rogue River Indians and Their Relations with the Whites*, Master's Thesis, University of Oregon, Eugene, OR, 1943,

Rowntree, Lester. *Flowering Shrubs of California.* Stanford University Press, Stanford University, CA, 1939.

Sampson, Arthur W., Agnes Chase, and Donald W. Hedrick. "California Grasslands and Range Forage Grasses," Bulletin 724, California Agricultural Experiment Station, University of California, Berkeley, CA, May 1951.

Sapir, Edward. "Takelma Texts," Anthropological Publications of the University Museum, Volume II, No.1, University of Pennsylvania, Philadelphia, PA, 1909.

Saunders, Charles Francis. *Western Wild Flowers and Their Stories*, Doubleday, Doran & Co. Garden City, NY, 1933.

Schwartz, Earl Albert. "Blood Money: The Rogue River Indian War and Its Aftermath, 1850–1986" Doctoral Dissertation, 1991.

Seevers, Joan and Darren Borgias. "Oregon Plants, Oregon Places: Upper and Lower Table Rocks, Jackson County," *Kalmiopsis*, Journal of the Native Plant Society or Oregon, V3 1993.

Seevers, Joan. Personal Communication, 1993. Medford District Botanist with the Bureau of Land Management, and member of the Table Rock Stewardship Committee.

Smith, Karen. Personal Communication, 1993. Special Projects Manager, Jackson County Public Works and Parks. Past member of the Lower Table Rock Stewardship Committee.

Smith, Lois. Personal Communication, 1992. Resident of Table Rock community and Audubon Society Member. Participated on initial Table Rock and Kelly Slough Study Committee, Member of the Table Rock Stewardship Committee, led interpretive walks for school children and TNC/BLM for many years.

Spellenberg, Richard. *The Audubon Society Field Guide to North American Wildflowers: Western Region*, Alfred A. Knopf, New York, NY, 1979.

St. John, Alan D. *Knowing Oregon Reptiles.* Booklet prepared for the Oregon Reptile Education Department, Salem Audubon Society, OR, 1980.

Stechman, John V. *Common Western Range Plants.* Vocational Education Productions, California Polytechnic State University, San Luis Obispo, CA, 1986.

Stubbendieck, J., Stephan Hatch, Kathie Kjar. *North American Range Plants.* University of Nebraska Press, Lincoln, NB, 1982.

Sutton, Jack. *Indian Wars of the Rogue River.* Klocker Printery, Medford, OR, 1969.

Table Rock and Kelly Slough Study Committee. Letters and minutes, November 1973–February 1974.

Walling, A.G. *History of Southern Oregon.* House of A.G. Walling, Portland, OR, 1884.

Walsh, Frank K. *Indian Battles Along The Rogue River: 1855-56*, Te-Cum-Tom Publications, Grants Pass, OR, 1972.

Weatherford, Mark V. "Rogue River Indian War," Unpublished Manuscript—no date.

Whittlesey, Rhonda. *Familiar Friends Northwest Plants*, Rose Press, Portland, OR, 1985.

Wilkerson, James A. *Medicine For Mountaineering*, The Mountaineers, Seattle, WA, 1985.

Wilkes, Charles. *Narrative of the United States Exploring Expedition*, Volume 5 of 5, Philadelphia, PA, 1849.

INDEX

Farewell. Kelly Hilyard and Chris Reyes, Upper Table Rock.